Dissolving Boundaries:
Toward An Integrative Curriculum

DISSOLVING BOUNDARIES:
TOWARD AN INTEGRATIVE CURRICULUM

Edward N. Brazee
Jody Capelluti

National Middle School Association

nmsa ®

NATIONAL MIDDLE SCHOOL ASSOCIATION

Ed Brazee, a former middle school teacher and team leader is a professor of education at the University of Maine in Orono. Jody Capelluti, a former middle school principal, is a professor at the University of Southern Maine in Gorham. Both Dr. Brazee and Dr. Capelluti are active leaders in efforts to advance the middle school movement and particularly to reform the middle school curriculum.

NMSA is grateful to the authors for organizing and developing this timely monograph, which becomes a significant addition to the growing body of literature on curriculum integration.

ISBN 1-56090-090-3

TABLE OF CONTENTS

ACKNOWLEDGEMENTS

We are indebted to the teachers and principals in the schools who shared their work with us. We commend their courage to make changes in the face of many obstacles. Changing what and how we teach is not easy work and we are grateful for their pioneering efforts.

In particular, we express our gratitude to Terry Depres and the Ashland Middle School faculty, Judith Bossie, Mary Bilodeau-Callan, Charlene Carper, John Kraljic, Laura Boutilier, Camille Barr, Sue Carol Thompson, Carol Stewart, Tonya Buckingham, Joann Hauser, and Karen Nelson for the leadership and the support they provided. Their involvement in the change process was crucial. Their willingness to share their successes and learnings was exemplary. And to the teachers whose dedication, perseverance, energy, and commitment resulted in new knowledge being added to the field, we say thanks. Without their strong belief in this work nothing would have been accomplished.

We express our great thanks to Dot Kelley, Vicki Schmidt, and Dianne Avery for their patience with our many revisions and their thoughtful support for our writing. Thanks as well to Mary Mitchell of NMSA for her careful and creative work in formatting this book for printing.

We would be remiss if we did not acknlwledge the previous work in this area by John Lounsbury, Gordon Vars, Connie Toepfer, Chris Stevenson, John Arnold, and Jim Beane. Our own work has been greatly influenced by their research and scholarship. A special word of commendation goes to Jim Beane for his inspiration, guidance, and always insightful thoughts on all aspects of learning.

To John Lounsbury, our editor, whose support and encouragement made this book possible, we express appreciation. John constantly reminded us that our work needed to be shared. His advice, not only as editor, but as an expert in this field, was invaluable. Rarely does one get the opportunity to work with an editor who is also an authority on the topic you are writing. John's willingness to share his knowledge, in a collegial manner, made the writing a pleasurable and unique learning experience.

From our children, Jeff and Chris, Jill and Andrew, two of whom were not long ago young adolescents and two who will soon be, came the inspiration for this work. And to our wives, Connie and Vanessa, whose experiences as reflective teachers helped us frame our thoughts, our love and thanks!

Ed Brazee
Jody Capelluti

October, 1994

FOREWORD   *James A. Beane*

Most curriculum design and change initiatives have followed one of two paths. The first is what we might call "grand narratives," designs meant for all places, all situations, and all people. At the end of this path is a homogenized school with a standardized, systematized, and aligned arrangement of subjects, texts, and tests. The social efficiency movement earlier in this century was a good example; we are still living with its legacy of Carnegie units of credit and seat time. Another good example, this one in our own time, is the chilling rhetoric and rapid approach of national standards, curriculum, and testing. This path almost always involves a linear model of top-down mandates for local implementation of separate subject content requirements.

The second path for curriculum design and change is neither linear nor top-down. Instead it involves two interacting dimensions. One is a definition of powerful principles that ought to guide the curriculum, the big ideas like democracy, self and social meaning, dignity, and so on. The other dimension is a diverse range of possibilities, locally developed, for bringing those principles to life. These two dimensions play off each other as we seek ways to bring the principles to life in our classrooms and continuously refine the principles on the basis of what we learn in our classrooms.

There is no set "curriculum," no recipe, no cookbook, no standardization, no alignment. Instead there is a set of guiding principles to give us direction and our own imaginations to create ways of bringing those principles to life. Thinking about curriculum design and change this way makes room for people to create their own local arrangements while sharing with others a commitment to common purposes.

This is why I called my own curriculum proposal "a" rather than "the" middle school curriculum and why I opened the revised edition with a more clearly defined statement of general guidelines for the curriculum (Beane, 1993). More importantly, however, is that this second path is where we locate the emerging literature on middle school curriculum that offers so much by way of promise and excitement. I am referring to the collections of real-life classroom and school stories about curriculum integration, collections like *Integrated Studies in the Middle Grades: Dancing Through Walls* (Stevenson and Carr, 1993), *Watershed: A Successful Voyage Into Integrative Learning* (Springer, 1994), *Moving Toward Whole Learning in the Middle School* (Pace, 1994), *Beyond Separate Subjects: Middle School Curriculum for the 21st Century* (Siu-Runyan and Faircloth, in press). And here is where we now place this new and important volume, *Dissolving Boundaries: Toward an Integrative Middle School Curriculum*. Those familiar with middle level education will certainly recognize the authors/editors, Ed Brazee and Jody Capelluti, as veterans of middle school curriculum reform just as they will recognize authors of the stories themselves from the programs of various national and state middle school conferences. We are lucky to now have these stories in print.

What is it that is so appealing about collections like this? Perhaps it is that these are stories about real classrooms and real schools written by real educators; these people *really* did this stuff. Perhaps it is the sense of adventure and courage involved in these curriculum projects. Perhaps it is that we are led to think about how we might have done things differently in one or another story and suddenly discover that we too have become part of this important curriculum work. Perhaps it is a sense that these people seem to have found, for the moment at least, a way of working with young people that is more satisfying than what happens in too many other schools. Perhaps it is all of these. Whatever the case, this is heady curriculum work and we are drawn to it in ways that commission reports, theoretical proposals, and similar fare from the usual educational literature simply cannot match.

Even as we honor the stories here, however, we must remember that an integrative curriculum is not simply about instructional methodology or technique. The larger purpose of this work involves the search for curriculum possibilities that are more democratic, more significant, more powerful, more engaging, and more respectful of the dignity and diversity of young people. Remembering this (or learning it for the first time) helps us to understand why Brazee and Capelluti press us to plan with young people, to distinguish between a clever "topic" and a socially significant "theme," and to spend time and intellect working through fundamental questions about curriculum in general and at the middle level in particular. So it is that this volume may be read not only for the exciting classroom and school accounts but for a well-crafted explanation of the theoretical concepts with which they intersect. Too many works about curriculum lack this balance. We should be charged extra for this book.

Moreover, having this account, and the others mentioned earlier, we are now in a position to see new questions beyond the ones we raised before there were even these stories.

What would happen if young people experienced these kinds of curriculum arrangements across several years?

Having experienced the richness of these curriculum experiences, what might be a next and more sophisticated set of questions or projects in which young people might be involved?

What would happen if the majority of middle school teachers undertook this kind of curriculum work, if a new generation of young people thought more critically, accessed information more easily, expected democratic participation, cared more deeply for others, demanded action on questions of justice, expected school to be about something of great significance?

What would happen to our high schools, to our workplaces, to our colleges, to our society?

Many might scoff at questions like these and say they are too "idealistic." But then, people scoffed only a few years ago when we asked whether there ought to be a new middle school curriculum.

In the end though, I must confess that there is something bittersweet about these stories, even about the whole integrative curriculum project. Anyone who has ever done this kind of curriculum work knows that all of these people have paid a price. Yes, they may make it sound easy or rattle off one success after another. But even if they never say so, we can be certain that there were sleepless nights, exhausting searches for resources, moments of terrifying uncertainty in the classroom, tense meetings with parents or school officials who could not see past the failed separate subject curriculum, and heartbreaking episodes in the coffee room under attack by those who were afraid that they might be expected to work this hard. Crossing the boundaries of subject areas is never easy, to say nothing of scaling the walls of tradition. This is not a kind of work meant for the fainthearted or marginally dedicated. We are lucky to have these stories and even luckier to call the authors our colleagues.

—James A. Beane
National-Louis University

I

CURRICULUM INTEGRATION: WHAT AND WHY

We can never again hope to design a curriculum to be required of everyone. A common content is simply no longer a valid goal for education.

—Arthur Combs

In times of change, learners shall inherit the earth while the learned are beautifully equipped for a world that no longer exists.

—Eric Hoffer

The Process of Curriculum Improvement

It's 1994 and

— our kids play with voice-controlled toys

— we can make a phone call and see the person we are talking to

— cars can give us directions in a strange city

— computers give us instant access to an encyclopedia if we press a key and,

— we can receive mail over the phone.

Yet, the school program is essentially the same as it was 25, even 50 years ago. For example, teachers still work predominantly in isolation from each other; the separate subject approach still dominates curriculum delivery; students are placed in rigid tracks/groups with varying expectations for achievement; and students are passive recipients of information, often seeing little or no application to the world they live in outside of school.

Personal lives have drastically changed during these decades; yet, what our students experience within our schools has changed very little. Why is it we are able to make successful and significant changes in our personal and corporate lives yet find changing what and how schools teach so difficult? Almost without exception, school improvement meets resistance even from those who teach in these schools. If we are to have any chance at successfully improving the curriculum, then an examination of issues surrounding the concept of change is fundamental. What can we glean from the literature to assist us in understanding the obstacles and help us remove these barriers? What do we know about teacher beliefs and administrative roadblocks concerning change?

Muncey and McQuillan (1993) discuss the preliminary findings of a five year study of Sizer's Coalition of Essential Schools, and raise the issue that there are some staff who want to make changes and still maintain the status quo. Other staff felt that society needed to change—not schools. If this would occur, then successful teaching and learning would happen.

Lewins (1951), recognized as a pioneer in understanding the process of change, talks about the need to unfreeze old patterns of behavior before moving to new ones. This unfreezing is caused by opposing forces exerting various amounts of pressure. Only when there is an imbalance of pressure will change occur. For example, despite tremendous societal change, the voice for maintaining the status quo of schools is stronger than the one to alter it; hence, change does not occur.

People don't necessarily resent the notion of change but rather they resent loss or the possibility of loss.

Capelluti (1990) notes that educators sometimes fight change because it forces them to give up practices that are familiar and occasionally successful. This challenge to the status quo results in a fear of losing what they already have. Burke (1982) argues that people don't necessarily resent the notion of change but rather they resent loss or the possibility of loss. Therefore, a redefinition of the status quo is needed (Capelluti, 1990).

For restructuring efforts to be successful there must be personal as well as philosophical changes (Thompson and Thompson, 1992). The question becomes, "How can you make changes and still maintain the status quo?"

James Belasco (1991) compares organizations to elephants in that both learn through conditioning. He talks about how young elephants are shouldered with heavy chains and tied to stakes that are deeply rooted in the ground. They learn that they cannot move far from the stakes. When they get older, although certainly forceful enough to rip the stake out of the ground, they do not. They, in fact, are no longer tied to a stake, but only have a small metal bracelet around one leg. Belasco, of course, refers to the notion that organizations are bound by earlier constraints, even successes. Still there is hope.

Yet when the circus tent catches on fire—and the elephant sees the flames with his own eyes and smells the smoke with its own nostrils—it forgets its old conditions and changes. Your task: set a fire so your people see the flames with their own eyes and smell the smoke with their own nostrils without burning the tent down. And anyone can set the fire at any level in the organization (p. 18).

Belasco further discusses the importance of establishing an urgency to change and states, "First, create the need to change, remove the rewards for present behavior. Empower people to want to change" (p. 19).

Thomas Romberg (1993), who chaired the landmark report *Curriculum and Evaluation Standards for School Mathematics,* talks about that committee's recommendations going beyond the traditional separate subject approach to teaching. Romberg also notes that mathematics should be studied in "living contexts that are meaningful to learners, including their language, cultures, and everyday lives, as well as their school based experiences" (p. 1). He goes on to state that the biggest obstacle to change for teachers, administrators, and parents "is the threat to school routines that are based on existing architecture, organization, and management" (p. 2).

English and Hill (1990) state that change is fundamentally a change in people. They point out that, "Principals must try to understand the agenda of each person in the school... and their need for some control and authority in the school" (p.35).

Changing the curriculum is a difficult process, one that is highly personal (Capelluti & Brazee, 1993b). "Such change assuredly requires a fundamental shift in individual beliefs about what the curriculum should be and how it can best be experienced. Therefore, any attempts at altering past curriculum must involve an extensive examination of a number of fundamentally held beliefs before something new can be explored" (p. 25).

Changing the curriculum is a difficult process, one that is highly personal.

Redefining the status quo

If curriculum change is really systemic change, and change is highly personal, how do we develop strategies to overcome what appears to be formidable and conflicting obstacles? The point is that we must begin by acknowledging that schools are not entities separate from the individual. Organizations are made up of a collection of individuals, although it would appear, in some instances, that this concept gets lost. Organizational learning can be all-encompassing and in fact a major inhibitor of change. We need to understand the many overall complexities related to schools and learn from those individuals who have successfully altered the organization by redefining the status quo.

How do you change the curriculum

To change the curriculum, one must create a need and a sense of urgency for change. To create this sense of urgency we need to redefine success and rethink failure. For example, are the assumptions on which school curriculum is

To change the curriculum, one must create a need and a sense of urgency for change.

now based still applicable? If a purpose of the curriculum is preparation for successful participation in the adult world, then, is the definition of success the same as it was twenty-five years ago? This does not necessarily mean that our programs in the past have been unacceptable. What it means is the beliefs upon which schools were based in the past no longer apply because present and future needs have significantly changed.

Supporting this premise is the report of the Sandia Strategic Studies Center. This study examined and analyzed local, state, and national education systems for the U.S. government. Robert Huelskamp (1993), reporting on their findings, states that on all academic measures they found steady or slight improvement. Although these test results are good news, he notes that it may be unimportant because, "...even if a particular measure is appropriate, steady, or slightly improving, these test results may not be adequate to meet future societal needs in an increasingly competitive world" (p. 719). Although the results may be encouraging, they are irrelevant if we are using outdated standards. If we would not accept medical treatment that people received even ten years ago, why would we expect students to accept an educational system that is fundamentally the same as it was seventy-five years ago?

The sense of urgency may be easier to create than the sense of needing to change. Some might argue that although they can accept in part the urgency argument, they are unsure of changing because of a lack of understanding about how to do it. Others may be concerned that they won't be supported or express a real feeling that they are overwhelmed and overworked now. Some would ask how can they possibly do something different while maintaining a sense of equilibrium in the classroom and personally? Others may wonder whether the risk will be accepted and rewarded.

Fullen & Hargraves (1991) believe that most attempts at school reform don't succeed. They cite the tendency to look for structural solutions to problems which rarely address issues of instruction and teacher development. To support this premise one only has to look at schedule changes in schools. Attempts at instituting block scheduling at the middle level and more recently changing high school classes to eighty minutes, for example, were made in many schools with little or no instructional assistance given to teachers. The assumption is that longer time periods, not different teaching and learning strategies, are needed. In other words, if the organizational structure were different, students would learn more. Fullen & Hargraves also conclude that not only do many change strategies fail but they tend to alienate teachers from participation in future reform efforts. Often attempts have failed because teachers have not had meaningful involvement and, as a result, there has been little change to the classroom.

The reforms of the 80s clearly taught us that top down policy mandates did little to change the outcome of education. To not involve those most affected by the mandates, namely teachers and students, in the decision-making process, is almost to guarantee failure. Hence, we now see guarded and cautious enthusiasm for newly posed concepts of collaborative decision-making, site-based management, and teacher empowerment.

> **To not involve those most affected by the mandates in the decision-making process, is almost to guarantee failure.**

Change is a highly personal experience. Schools don't change, individuals do. If we are to significantly alter our way of doing business in schools, then we must begin by examining our beliefs.

New beliefs about teaching and learning are needed

We believe that changing the curriculum and subsequently how it is delivered demand a change in beliefs. Without this philosophical research, no serious reform can take place. What new beliefs are needed to reshape practices?

Belief 1: All children can succeed and should be held to high expectations.

At present, because of the practice of tracking, success is essentially limited to a select group of students. In fact, to ensure this, students in some tracks can only achieve goals to a certain level. In high schools, this is taken a step further with the designation of leveled courses. This practice considers some courses more rigorous and demanding and they are assigned a higher level than some other courses. Chemistry, for example, might be assigned a level IV designation while Consumer Math might be a level I. This practice ensures that students labeled upper level will always be in the top ten (and valedictorians and salutatorians) while the general student is relegated to the bottom third of the class even if they both receive all A's. To further demonstrate the system's restrictive policy, courses which concentrate on doing or producing art are less important than courses which stress learning about art. Art Appreciation, for example, is given higher level designations than those courses that produce art. This leads students to conclude that looking at art and trying to figure out what the artist is trying to tell us is more difficult and important than the act of producing the art that is to be viewed.

Assuredly then, one must develop a set of beliefs and practices that shows students that success is expected of all, not just a few, and that everyone has access to the total curriculum. No longer can we have a series of separate curriculums, that, in fact, guarantee future failure for some students. Without certain courses they are denied admission to opportunities for a future education.

Belief #2: Team work and individual effort should be rewarded.

At present, the system is based on individual success. Schooling is competitive not collaborative. Students are pitted against each other, realizing that their success is, in fact, not only based on how they do, but on how poorly someone else does. Schools say that they want students to work cooperatively but the reality of rewards doesn't reflect this. One only has to look at team sports. Why do we give most valuable player awards on team sports? Do we think kids are naïve? We tell them how important the team is, that they need to be a team player; yet, at the annual awards banquet we give individual awards. Something is wrong. Businesses want team players. Recently, a teacher in a vocational high school told me that the CEO of a prestigious furniture maker told him to only send team players for interviews. If a function of school is to prepare students for success in the workplace, shouldn't we prepare them with skills they will need. A recent review of the Sunday *Boston Globe* and *New York Times* classified ads revealed the following statements about job requirements.

> Director of Marketing Communications—*who will create, develop and lead a **team**.*
> Emergency Room Technician—*become part of a **team**.*
> Copywriter—*the ability to work well in a **team**-environment.*
> Senior Programmer Analyst —*a willingness and interest in being a **team** player.*
> Sales Manager—*Must be a **team** player...with an entrepreneurial spirit.*
> Billing Clerk—***team**work and attention to detail a must.*
> Staff Pharmacist—*You will be enjoying the camaraderie of a cohesive **team** atmosphere.*
> Senior System Analyst—*creating an atmosphere in which you can reach your own goals, while we as a **team** reach ours.*
> Executive Secretary—*...seeking a few individuals to take part in our success and enjoy our **team** environment.*
> Clinical Nurse—*must be able to work in a **team** approach.*
> Director of Corporate Relations—***team** building skills are considered extremely important.*
> Attorney—*Join our dynamic **team**.*

If we want our children to be prepared for the workplace, isn't it obvious that schools must begin teaching people how to work together? Employers think it is.

Belief #3: Learning should be relevant and responsive to the learner at the time it occurs.

Many students learn content and skills in the vague hope that someday they will be able to use them. Or they learn content and skills because it is a hurdle to overcome en route to the next step. They wait patiently for the real world where they are told it will be meaningful. Curriculum is usually viewed as something to cover and get through. It is not recognized as inherently enjoyable but rather is regarded as work that needs to be done. It is often seen through comments such as "we need to cover this today," and "if we can get through this before the end of the period, you can work on projects that interest you." Skills, knowledge, and content should not be taught in isolation from practice.

Recent curriculum reform efforts have questioned the merits of covering content at the risk of never learning something in depth. A glance at curriculum goals written since the release of *A Nation at Risk* (Carnegie Council, 1983) would reveal that a significant amount of information has been added. This increase in coverage expectation only adds to teachers' frustration and students' confusion as to what really needs to be learned. Teachers and students are typically not part of this decision-making process. The curriculum wasn't theirs. At best, what results from this type of system are students who have become good consumers of information, rather than active learners exploring their own questions about what is relevant to be learned.

Belief #4 - An integrative approach to curriculum rather than separate subject isolation makes sense.

Currently, most schools organize the curriculum in a way that separates disciplines. There are few or no formal structures in place that allow students to see relationships between subjects. Students are sent to rooms where a subject is discussed and then after forty-five minutes go to another room where another subject is discussed. This instructional strategy happens each period of the day for the school year and is repeated in subsequent years. Students encounter none or only sporadic experiences that make learning whole. If there is overlap, it is usually a chance occurrence. The rationale behind the departmentalized approach is that disciplines can best be learned in isolation from one another and that more content can be learned if it is segregated. Still we expect students as adults and lifelong learners to solve problems by using disciplines simultaneously, when in fact they have had no formal training for doing so.

What is integrative curriculum? We have written previously that:

> Integrative curriculum is based on a holistic view of learning and recognizes the necessity for learners to see the big picture rather than to require learning be divided into small pieces. Integrative curriculum ignores traditional subject lines while exploring questions which are most relevant to students. As a result, it is both responsive to students' needs and intellectual because it focuses on helping learners use their minds well. There is in fact, no one integrative curriculum, but rather principles of teaching and learning which guide the development of integrative curriculum in diverse settings (Brazee & Capelluti, 1993c).

Much, if not most, of the content and skills in traditional curriculum are found in integrative curriculum approaches. What is different is that the knowledge, skills, and attitudes needed for success in tomorrow's world will be presented and studied in a context that is relevant to the student.

Typical school curriculums are based on the premise that the subjects should be separated with no connections between disciplines planned. Fogarty (1991) refers to this as the Fragmented Model of Curriculum Design. She states: "This model views the curriculum through a periscope, offering one sighting at a time: one directed focus as a single discipline and, typically, the major academic areas are math, science, language arts, and social studies. Each is seen as a pure entity in and of itself. Relationships between subject areas—physics and chemistry, for example— are only implicitly indicated" (p. 62).

Integrative curriculum attempts to dissolve subject boundaries, assist students in making learning connections between disciplines, and helps them see learning in a holistic rather than fragmented way. The stories in chapters 4-10 provide descriptions of real and successful attempts at doing such.

New beliefs about how early adolescents learn focus on students being able to identify and solve problems (Brazee and Capelluti, 1993b).

> Thematic units in middle schools and beyond must be experiences in inquiry...we must use what we know about learning by planning activities which are relevant to students' lives, allow students to study, explore, and create knowledge around issues that are real in today's world and which need real solutions. Such activities should allow students to participate as active, not passive, learners, as problem creators and problem solvers. Finally, and obviously,

given such a problem focus, skills, knowledge and attitudes need to be used in compelling and meaningful contexts, not in isolation" (p. 28).

An integrative approach that moderates the separation of subjects, and involves students as responsible and collaborative learners may provide the instructional model for meaningful learning. The teacher does not abdicate the responsibility for the curriculum but rather works with students to create experiences in which students explore their interests and needs within the overall standards set by the district. Curriculum development of this nature places the emphasis for decision-making where it should be—with students and teacher. The student becomes an active participant, learning from teachers and other students, community members, and resources as well. Serious attempts are made to make learning functional to the learner. Expectations are high, success is expected for everyone and access to the full curriculum is available to all. Experiences with integrative approaches have shown that this approach has resulted in increased student achievement and enjoyment of learning.

For some schools these paradigm shifts in beliefs will be difficult. Teachers and students will have trouble adjusting to new expectations and role definitions. New conditions for teaching and learning will test the fabric of past assumptions. Some who have been successful in the old structure will resist the change because of a loss of prestige, comfort level, or because old habits are difficult to change.

We believe the new belief strategies and accompanying practices will occur. Why will it occur? Because teachers who are cognizant of the developmental needs of early adolescents and aware of the skills needed for these students to be successful in the future, realize that such a proposal makes sense. In fact, to do otherwise, to maintain the status quo, only assures that our students will not be prepared for success as adults. Schools must keep pace with the rapidly changing needs of society and must reflect the best of what we know about effective instructional and organizational practices for early adolescents.

To maintain the status quo only assures that our students will not be prepared for success as adults.

Using an integrated approach to curriculum planning and instructional delivery provides the design needed to allow the original goals of the middle level movement to be reached. It recognizes and honors their uniqueness, is developmentally appropriate, and intellectually challenging. *An Agenda for Excellence at the Middle Level* (Council on Middle Level Education, 1985) states it clearly and forcefully:

Because we cannot teach them all they need to know, we must teach them how to learn and how to adjust their lives to the change that will surround them. To do this, we must provide high quality intellectual climates in our middle level schools and foster the development of adaptive skills that our students can use throughout their lives (p.1-2).

The stories of schools, found later in this book, provide helpful information and guidelines for teachers and schools beginning to move from a single, separate subject-based instructional approach to an integrative approach to learning. →

2   A RATIONALE FOR CURRICULUM INTEGRATION

The middle level movement has been the single most enduring and influential educational innovation of the 20th century (Lounsbury, 1984). Until recently, the middle school movement has largely been a grass roots movement led by teachers who knew that traditional junior high schools did not provide the type of school needed for 10-14 year olds. Paradoxically, the middle level in the K-12 continuum is still one of the best-kept secrets in the United States. In spite of the numerous positive effects of middle school philosophy on school practice since 1960, most improvements have centered around improving school climate and changing aspects of school organization, while the core of the middle level program, the curriculum, has remained largely untouched.

For example, when talking with teachers about how their schools are developmentally responsive, it is instructive that they mention advisor-advisee programs, intramurals, exploratory programs, special weekend excursions, and the like; but they rarely refer to activities which are a part of the normal school day, and hence, the conventional curriculum. It appears that the interesting and engaging activities in middle level schools take place before and after "regular" classes are dismissed.

The first rumblings of interest in addressing the fundamental curriculum questions in middle level schools began only in the late 1980s, so for the first three decades of the middle school movement, the curriculum question was the "absent presence" (Beane, 1990a). In spite of the many successes of the past thirty years, schools and curriculum theorists have ignored the tough curriculum issues as they confronted problems in climate, guidance, and school organization. Typically, schools attempting to adopt a more middle school-like philosophy implemented advisory, exploratory, and intramural programs as evidence that they were, indeed, middle schools.

13

While thousands of middle level schools have successfully adopted such programs, and while these programs have benefited even more thousands of young adolescents, this has not adequately kept the promise of the middle level school to provide a program responsive to young adolescents' needs. As important as these programs are, they are "add-ons," and exist *outside* the curriculum concerns of the traditional four academic subjects. As such they are seen as parallel tracks, not overlapping or influencing the "close the door, teacher-centered, textbook-dominated curriculum." More importantly, this limited view about what middle level schools can and should be has severely hindered programs in middle level schools across the country. It is to this issue that we turn our attention in this chapter.

Don't confuse *academic* with *intellectual*

Because the discussion about curriculum has been almost non-existent, the status quo, "teach what we have always taught" mentality has predominated. In short, few have made serious inquiries about what the curriculum should be.

Understanding the difference between what is academic and what is intellectual is crucial.

One of the key issues in any discussion of curriculum reform is "it was good enough for me...." This way of thinking is exceedingly difficult to dispute, especially with those who feel strongly about the conventional curriculum *they* experienced. Often underlying this type of thinking is a fundamental confusion about what is academic and what is intellectual. Understanding the difference is crucial!

"Academic," in K-12 school terms, refers to the subject areas of English, science, mathematics, and social studies. These subjects are often juxtaposed against other "non-academic" subjects like physical education, band, music, art, home economics and similar courses; the assumption is that "academic" subjects are more important, more rigorous, and more challenging and have a higher status in the school. In debates about the purposes and function of schools, "academics" are the "basics" often returned to. "Academic" courses are also those which receive the highest recognition and the most support, financial and otherwise in schools. When economic times are difficult, no one talks about cutting mathematics, science, or language arts.

Used in this way, we *ASSUME* that the subjects referred to as "academic" are ultimately more important; we assume that the content, knowledge, skills, and attitudes which comprise these subjects have a higher value for students. Yet many "non-academic" subjects are as or more rigorous than the "academic" subjects. The assumption is that because students put in their time in classes called English, science, or mathematics, they are academically challenged. We should be less concerned with a narrowly defined set of courses which are referred to as "academic" and more interested in intellectual development, where students are challenged to use their minds and abilities to perform important work, no matter what the subject matter or title of the class. Our goal should be intellectually rigorous work, wherever that occurs in the school.

We should be less concerned with narrow academic courses and more concerned with challenging students to use their minds and perform important tasks.

One final assumption here is worth noting. The traditional "academic" versus "non-academic" argument is predicated on an either-or fallacy. That is, if you want to be an academically rigorous school, then you concentrate on traditional "high status" disciplines. Similarly, if you place value on other ways of knowing and other types of knowledge, the arts, music, practical arts, technology, physical fitness, and many others, then it is often assumed you are not serious about "academic" learning. Why can't we have both?

What is the curriculum today?

The middle level curriculum landscape has changed dramatically in the past five years. Beginning with the publication of James Beane's *From Rhetoric to Reality* in 1990, the curriculum conversation as it has come to be called, has quite literally exploded. Much more than just another element on the list of middle level characteristics, serious and reasoned consideration of what the middle level curriculum should be (and *how* it should be) is of utmost concern, especially to those teachers in schools who have implemented conventional middle school elements and now realize that that is not enough.

As both the past and future curriculums are examined, other typical middle level practices are being examined as a result of the focus on curriculum. For example, many middle level schools are questioning their separate advisor-advisee programs when those functions are incorporated by teams with a strong integrative curriculum. Similarly, the roles and functions of conventional interdisciplinary teams undergo scrutiny in light of new possibilities and demands brought about by integrative curriculum. Studying curriculum *forces* schools to take a long, hard look at their responses in all areas.

Until recently, school-wide curriculum development had not been high on the agenda of middle level schools, perhaps because they needed to concentrate on other more immediate and achievable goals. Beane (1990a), suggests that if the curriculum question had received attention earlier in the middle school movement, and serious questioning about the continuation of the traditional subjects had occurred, the movement might not have survived.

Or perhaps schools have been unwilling to deal with school-wide curriculum development because of problems encountered in coordinating, articulat-

Curriculum is highly personal and highly political, and making changes from the conventional curriculum is very difficult.

ing, and implementing mission and philosophy. Although many schools would not admit it, tinkering with school climate and organization, by instituting interdisciplinary teams and by changing the schedule, is much easier than looking carefully at what the curriculum should be. Curriculum is highly personal and highly political, and making changes from the conventional curriculum is very, very difficult.

The general state of curriculum development at the middle level compared to what it could and should be is disappointing, because it certainly has not kept pace with what it could be. As Joan Lipsitz noted in her classic study, *Successful Schools For Young Adolescents* (1984), "translating philosophy into curriculum is the most difficult feat for schools to accomplish. The translation to climate and organizational structure appears to be much easier for these schools than the translation of purpose into curriculum."

There is little consolation in the fact that school-wide curriculum development in elementary and high schools is no more advanced. The fact is, thirty years after the beginning of the middle school movement, schools have made far too little progress in developing legitimate, school-wide curricula. And while teachers have always developed new curricula in their own classes or within interdisciplinary teams, school-wide curriculum planning, where all elements of the school program are considered, has not been a typical activity in most middle level schools (Cawelti, 1988).

More recently, serious study has sought to answer the question, "What should the middle school curriculum be?" A myriad of other queries have spawned from that question—questioning all past practices and even the wisdom of conventional middle school dogma. While not antithetical to suggestions of practice and research literature, the best work in curriculum pushes conventional middle level thinking to new limits. Practices of adding an advisory program, forming interdisciplinary teaching teams, or adding exploratory courses do not themselves make a school responsive to the needs of young adolescents. While veteran teachers might find this "new" curriculum direction somewhat disconcerting, like changing the rules in the middle of the game, in the long run they will recognize the importance of curriculum as the central focus. Seen another way, this emphasis is not really curriculum improvement, but curriculum planning, for we are finally committing to what the curriculum should be for the first time!

Current influences

As noted earlier, the publication of James Beane's monograph *A Middle School Curriculum: From Rhetoric to Reality* (1990a) served as the rallying point for what is now known as the curriculum conversation. For many veteran middle level schools, the organizational responses of new schedules and add-on programs was not enough; the intuitive "feel" that middle level teachers have about what works and what doesn't caused these schools to look at the curriculum as the next critical focus. Subsequently, many veteran schools have begun serious curriculum work. The level of activity in middle level curriculum during the past five years has been nothing short of astounding. Always careful not to offer a prescription for solving the curriculum questions, new curriculum theorists in universities and schools have instead challenged teachers to ask and answer the all-important questions of curriculum development; for many, the disparate pieces of middle school philosophy are meshing.

The level of activity in middle level curriculum during the past five years has been nothing short of astounding.

Other sources have contributed to the conversation as well. The work of the Middle Level Curriculum Project (MLCP) has provided many insights into what the middle level curriculum can be (McDonough, 1991). This group of teachers, administrators, and university professors was one of the original groups to study the curriculum issue. They reminded us of the serious nature of young adolescent thinking and how desperately 10-14 year olds wish to make sense of their own lives as well as investigate questions about the larger world.

The National Middle School Association has taken a substantial lead in the conversation through two themed issues of the *Middle School Journal* (November 1992, January 1993), *Readings in Middle School Curriculum* (1993), and several other monographs dealing with curriculum, and in developing the statement "Middle Level Curriculum: A Work in Progress" (1993; 1994), the initial curriculum position paper of NMSA. This position paper clearly and forthrightly states types of curricular experiences young adolescents should have, and concludes with a list of "counter-productive conditions which should be phased out. Among the latter are: curricula consisting chiefly of separate subjects, skills taught in isolation, faculty organized by departments, and situations where students are labeled and tracked into rigid ability groups. Other state and regional organizations, like the New England League of Middle Schools, have also written their own position statements about curriculum which echo similar themes of integration across disciplines, student involvement, and the importance of local curriculum planning.

Most important are the thousands of schools, teams and individual teachers who are working to provide a curriculum responsive to young adolescents' needs. These risk-takers are adding immeasurably to our knowledge about what works and what doesn't and are setting a curriculum standard which elementary and high schools will soon follow. There are excellent examples of curriculum integration in every state in this country, and seven of their stories are included in this book.

Assumptions about the middle level curriculum

But the curriculum issue is much more complex than answering the question, "What should we teach?" It is more involved than a team deciding to use an interdisciplinary or multidisciplinary unit by setting aside the "regular curriculum" before school vacations or at the end of the school year. Conventional middle school curricula consists of courses, activities, and expectations; many exist, not for their inherent worth, but because they have always been there. Most curricula for middle school students are not based on what we know about young adolescents, principles of learning, the nature of various disciplines, or other important curriculum considerations. The "why fix it if it ain't broke" concept applies to middle level curriculum, but only if the IT (the curriculum) works correctly in the first place, and that has not always been the case.

For the middle level school to deal with curriculum as a legitimate part of total school development, those involved must understand the powerful impact of tradition and the traditional assumptions which limit thinking about curriculum. These assumptions are visible in common practices and expectations relative to curriculum and its ultimate support in middle level schools throughout the country (Brazee/Capelluti, 1992b).

Assumption #1—There is a curriculum which is the standard against which all others is measured. "If our school would use the right curriculum, our problems would be solved." Curriculum in this case is seen as static, not ever-changing to meet the needs of students, community, and teachers. It is also seen as originating from "experts" outside the local district, not from those most directly responsible for its development, young adolescents and their teachers.

Assumption #2—Not all areas of the curriculum have equal importance or value. Core, academic, or basics (usually language arts, social studies, science and mathematics) are regarded as more important than most other areas like home economics, foreign language, art, technology education, and music. And yet, it is those other areas that often supply a learning spark which the "core" subjects do not. More importantly, they represent other ways of knowing, of making sense of the world (Gardner,1983).

Assumption #3—Curriculum is a set of narrowly defined courses. In actuality, curriculum is all courses, learnings, activities, which collectively make up the school experience. Curriculum includes the planned and unplanned experiences which provide opportunities for learning. Extra-curricular or co-curricular activities are misnamed. They are a part of *the* curriculum of schools. Those involved in curriculum work have a larger vision of what schools can be, a vision larger than assignments, homework, and textbooks; a vision that curriculum is more than the sum of its parts.

Assumption #4—"The 'old style' curriculum was good enough for me, it should be good enough for my child." Very few people would accept medical care they received during their youth as good enough for them now. Very few would hire a lawyer whose practice had not been updated since 1945, but curiously many will not support a curriculum which is different from the one they experienced as students. Simply stated, the curriculum of most middle level schools prepares students for life in the United States 40 years ago, not for today, and certainly not for the world of tomorrow.

Assumption #5—Curriculum is too important to leave to teachers. Those most closely responsible for curriculum development in middle level schools are teachers and students, and yet we have not allowed them to use their expertise. We must allow teachers to use the knowledge of their students and the skills they have acquired to develop the most appropriate curriculum.

Unfortunately, these assumptions have severely limited thinking about the possibilities for curriculum development in middle level schools, and until recently, few people have asked serious questions about middle level curriculum development. Fortunately, the work of Stevenson, Lounsbury, Arnold, Beane, Toepfer and others (Dickinson, 1993) have stimulated our thoughts and actions. In the next section, we examine several of the current barriers to curriculum work, and then examine a vision of what middle level curriculum could be.

Understanding the barriers to curriculum work

If, as the literature and practices of middle level schools indicate, curriculum considerations have received scant attention, we must ask why this has happened. Challenging, or even talking about what the curriculum should be is often a nerve-wracking process, for the curriculum is personal to each of us. There is no question that changes in middle level schools have been for the most part limited to those areas, such as school climate and school organization, which affected teachers the least. They have accepted advisory programs, interdisciplinary teams, block schedules and other changes which made life more pleasant for students, but have not pushed ahead to make similar changes in the content of the curriculum.

Middle level transition activities have not usually required teachers to examine their fundamental beliefs about teaching and learning. When the typical middle school adopted middle level characteristics, they usually did so without asking teachers to change in any substantial way what they actually do for the majority of the day. Teachers were not required to utilize better ways of teaching, present all-new content, or base instruction on what young adolescents will need to know and be able to do in the future. In fact, many teachers have been pacified during middle school transition by administrators who said, in effect, "these changes will not affect how and what you teach"—and in many instances this was true. So hundreds of schools have made surface-level organizational changes which did not touch anyone's basic beliefs about what and how young adolescents learn!

A second major barrier is the influence of tradition on the school. Even allowing for some regional differences, the American school experience is more alike than different. This common school experience has caused millions of Americans to believe that all schooling must be similar to their own. Deviations from what they remember in their middle level (junior high school) years are scrutinized and often rejected as wrong.

Grammar study, as a major piece of middle school language arts, is a good example of the powerful role of tradition in the curriculum While extensive research indicates the folly of teaching grammar in isolation as a way of improving writing ability, grammar study in grades 6-8 continues to comprise a significant portion of the middle level language arts curricula. More importantly, it is a strong part of the *folklore* of what English (or language arts curriculum) should be. Adults and parents remember the hours spent and their struggles with Warriner's grammar book and become concerned if their own children don't repeat that process. In short, even if the experience was unpleasant, they remember grammar study and diagramming sentences and think that they are crucial to the language arts curriculum.

Arguably, the most influential barrier to change in middle level curriculum is the powerful and pervasive impact of high school expectations on middle school curriculum. One effect of the post-Sputnik educational reform movement was moving high school requirements and curriculum into the middle school. Moving a course from high school to the middle school without any adjustment causes an obvious mismatch if concepts or skills taught do not match the current intellectual functioning of young adolescents. A good example is algebra and to what extent it should be offered in the middle level school. In some schools, algebra is being forced into the eighth grade so that students have additional time in high school to take upper-level mathematics courses. Many students are not cognitively capable of either understanding or applying beginning algebra in eighth grade (Prevost, 1988). Those who *are* capable, however, should have an opportunity to study it.

> **Arguably, the most influential barrier to change in middle level curriculum is the powerful and pervasive impact of high school expectations.**

The same issue arises with foreign language as it is pushed down into the middle school. Like tradition, the influence of the high school curriculum is not based on what is known about young adolescents nor is it based on what is best for them in the middle level school. The power of such barriers, however, should not be underestimated.

Why the separate subject approach does not work

Questioning the efficacy of the separate subject approach is certainly not a new concept, yet it is a central concept in the new curriculum conversation (Beane, 1990; Vars, 1993). Strong evidence suggests that the separate subject approach is as inappropriate for high school students as it is for middle level students, yet it continues to dominate the way curriculum is organized because it is so deeply rooted in our experience and in the structures which underlie the schooling system, including teacher certification, university preparation, textbook sales, and standardized testing. Unfortunately, it presents serious problems for students and teachers and is, in many ways, a barrier to effective learning.

Beane is very clear about the limitations of separate subjects as curriculum and in a reasoned and rational manner, systematically debunks the separate subject myth. "In other words, the subject approach is alien to life itself. Put simply, it is 'bad' learning theory." Readers who wish a fuller discussion of this topic should refer to his work. But it is important to remember that we cannot provide the justification for a new curriculum, merely by discrediting the current subject-centered curriculum.

Not surprisingly, the current work in curriculum is not newly invented. Indeed, integrative curriculum is firmly rooted in the Progressive Education era and is supported by a large body of research and literature. Gordon Vars (1992) has documented numerous studies which have demonstrated the efficacy of non-subject centered curriculum.

Perhaps the most comprehensive study of the separate subject-approach and its alternatives is the *Eight Year Study* (Aikin, 1942), in which graduates of thirty experimental high schools fared better in both academic and social measures in college than did matched peers from conventional subject-centered programs. Most startling was the finding that graduates from the six high schools that varied most radically from the subject approach, using a variety of integrated approaches, achieved higher ratings than all other students.

Why we need a new vision of the middle level curriculum

Let's talk about *THE* middle level curriculum. Not in the sense that there is one which can be replicated to insure a successful middle level school. Let's talk about Curriculum with a capital *C,* as the entire school program. Specifically, we must go beyond the narrow view of curriculum as language arts, mathematics, science and social studies. Music, art, home economics, technology education, foreign languages, physical education, and others are just as important to young adolescents as the traditional "academic" subjects and provide ways of knowing which are not evident in the traditional subjects.

Schools with exploratory programs often treat such programs as if they are outside the "academic" area. A course here and an activity there rarely offer students the exploratory opportunities they need and deserve. Generally, middle level schools have accommodated the need for exploration in the special areas, often called "non-academic" as opposed to the heart of the middle level curriculum—language arts, mathematics, science, and social studies (Brazee, 1987).

To date, most curricula for middle level schools have not been based on what we know about young adolescents, accepted principles of learning, the nature of the various disciplines, or other curriculum development considerations. We must begin to use what we know if we are to positively impact these young people.

To develop a more comprehensive view of curriculum, teachers, parents, students, and others must realize that there is no one *best* curriculum that solves all the curricular problems and meets everyone's needs. Although there are many sources available to assist in developing middle level curricula, it must ultimately be developed locally. And it is certainly much more than finding the best materials or the best textbook; it is the process of studying what is and what should be, based on a deep understanding of the nature of various types and kinds of knowledge, the needs of the students, and the expectations of the community. In spite of the lack of interest in the total middle level curriculum, there is a vast amount of information available to curriculum developers at the local level.

There is no one best curriculum that meets everyone's needs. Curriculum must ultimately be developed locally.

Are we preparing our youth for the 21st century?

Today's schools do not prepare our youth for current challenges, let alone prepare them for the world of tomorrow. Schools still employ the old industrial model which is as out-of-date in schools as it is in industry. Just as industries no longer use workers in large, impersonal, "cookie-cutter" jobs, schools must move away from this model, no matter how strongly it is supported by parents and the lay public.

The education and training that students now need to prepare themselves for the workplace is radically different from what business and industry expected of students only 20 years ago. Hoffmann (1991) of Champion International Corporation lends some insight to this question when he talks about what Champion looks for in a new employee. His company seeks to hire individuals who can:

1. communicate effectively—read, write, speak, and listen effectively;
2. work in a group structure as a contributing member of a team;
3. presently use or be able to be trained in technology;
4. solve problems and demonstrate critical thinking skills.

In 1991 the Department of Labor attempted to identify "the demands of the workplace and whether our young people are capable of meeting those demands." The Secretary's Commission on Achieving Necessary Skills (SCANS) report identified five competencies and a three-part foundation that lie at the heart of effective job performance (1991). The Workplace Know-How list from the SCANS report is provided on page 24.

This widely quoted report focuses on only one part of societal expectations for schools, preparation for the world of work, but it reiterates the emphasis that "good jobs will increasingly depend on people who can put knowledge to work."

Certainly, the expectations for future workers go well beyond the expectations of the conventional school curriculum. While the Sandia Report (Huelskamp, 1993) reminds us that the general public perception of U.S. students as deficient in basic skills is not true, that report also reminds us that the standards of 50 years ago are no longer accurate barometers of where students should be today! We obviously need young adolescents with strong basic skills, but they also need much more than that. There are clearly other equally important reasons to develop youth who are capable of thinking critically. An integrated curriculum produces learners who will add greatly to a democratic, humanitarian society, both locally and globally.

For the middle level curriculum, the status quo is not good enough, for it means that we are not just standing still, we are actually moving backwards. ➔

WORKPLACE KNOW-HOW

The know-how identified by SCANS is made up of five competencies and a three-part foundation of skills and personal qualities that are needed for solid job performance. These are:

WORKPLACE COMPETENCIES: Effective workers can productively use:

- **Resources**—They know how to allocate time, money, materials, space, and staff

- **Interpersonal skills**—They can work on teams, teach others, serve customers, lead, negotiate, and work well with people from culturally diverse backgrounds.

- **Information**—They can acquire and evaluate data, organize and maintain files, interpret and communicate, and use computers to process information.

- **Systems**—They understand social, organizational, and technological systems; they can monitor and correct performance; and they can design or improve systems.

- **Technology**—They can select equipment and tools, apply technology to specific tasks, and maintain and troubleshoot equipment.

FOUNDATION SKILLS: Competent workers in the high-performance workplace need:

- **Basic Skills**—reading, writing, arithmetic and mathematics, speaking, and listening.

- **Thinking Skills**—the ability to learn, to reason, to think creatively, to make decisions, and to solve problems

- **Personal Qualities**—individual responsibility, self-esteem and self-management, sociability, and integrity.

3

THE CURRICULUM CONTINUUM: MOVING WHERE WE NEED TO BE

Do these comments sound familiar?

We involve students and parents to a much greater extent than we used to.

Take it out of the box, dust it off, and plug it in. Now, it is ready to use in our school.

The student voice in curriculum is essential. While we don't expect students to initially choose topics like fractions, parts of speech, and causes of the Civil War, the issues and topics they select provide the framework for studying everything important.

We can't do that here! Modern Middle School can experiment with integrated curriculum, hands-on instruction and portfolios because they have the good kids, parental support, the smartest teachers, and administrative backing.

There is no doubt that our curriculum is more rigorous now. We have higher standards, we expect more of students and ourselves, and parents are beginning to see that the learning (and teaching) we use here is more effective than the traditional stuff they hold as important.

Listen, we just need to go back to what we used to do. We are too easy on the kids and there is too much fluff in the curriculum. Let's get back to the 3 Rs.

The comments above represent two opposing viewpoints frequently heard today in discussion about middle level curriculum. While some still view curriculum as rigid and stagnant, more and more educators are beginning to view curriculum as an ongoing, ever-changing process. Fortunately, both the level and content of the curriculum conversation have changed dramatically in recent years now outpacing discussions on organizational and school climate issues which preoccupied us for so long. More and more middle schools have begun the process of change and entered into conversations on how to accomplish these changes. For many the question now is, "How can I make my middle level curriculum more interdisciplinary?"

But here is the rub. For some, curriculum has become another "essential component" of successful middle schools, sitting alongside exploratories, advisor/advisee, and interdisciplinary teams. We have lost sight of the fact that advisory and exploratory programs, interdisciplinary teams, and other common middle school elements are *responses* to particular needs of young adolescents; these programs are important only as they are developmentally responsive. And finally, we can't talk about curriculum as separate from those other components mentioned above.

To place curriculum as a separate category on the list of middle school elements, does not recognize the effect curriculum has on every other aspect of the school.

This new-found interest in curriculum does not mean that it should take its place on the middle school component checklist, because curriculum is all-encompassing. Every aspect of the middle school is curriculum. Before and after school, on the playground, in the lunchroom, on the bus to and from school, interscholastic sports, drama, and music are all essential elements of middle school curriculum. To place icurriculum as a separate category on the list of middle school elements, does not recognize the effect it has on every other aspect of the school.

To view interdisciplinary curriculum as the next (important) middle level component misses the point entirely. In attempting to meet the "spirit" of this new focus on interdisciplinary curriculum, several scenarios are being played out in schools. The first is to include one or two interdisciplinary units into the "regular" curriculum sometime during the year. Some middle level teams are searching for pre-written interdisciplinary units to cut down on preparation time for new units. Other teams are building in a set number of interdisciplinary units, which are completed at predictable times of the year, prior to holidays or at the end of the year.

In some schools, those teachers who have been successful at interdisciplinary units report that they are "doing Beane" (or worse yet, "did Beane") or have adopted the "Beane model" as their curriculum. Others, building on the work of

Heidi Hayes Jacobs (1989a), readily adopted an integrated model and placed that model on top of the conventional curriculum. While most of these efforts recognize a sincere desire to move toward curricular integration for all the right reasons, this type of shotgun approach is based on insufficient knowledge of both young adolescents and curriculum improvement. A real danger is that an unplanned approach to curriculum development will result in far fewer sustainable programs.

The notion of creating our own curriculum is not an easy concept to understand, especially in this time of state mandates, national standards, and recommendations from every imaginable source on what public school teachers should teach. If it were, more schools would be further along the road to defining the curriculum needs of their students.

The notion of creating our own curriculum is not an easy concept to understand.

In their inspiring book, *Integrated Studies in the Middle Grades: Dancing Through Walls*, Stevenson and Carr (1993), encourage us to go beyond the curriculum ideas about which Vermont teachers write, "we invite all readers who know the exigencies of educating children in transition and who wish for more than the ordinary, to consider our experience, then create their own"(p. 4).

In *Watershed: A Successful Voyage Into Integrative Learning*, Mark Springer tells of the seven year odyssey into integrated curriculum that he and his teammate have taken. A journey characterized by many rapids and waterfalls, not the least of which are internal to the school itself, *Watershed* is a marvelous work that chronicles the year to year successes and struggles of two teachers and 40 kids whose curriculum is built around the watershed in southeastern Pennsylvania. Despite clear evidence of the program's success, the two teachers are clearly disappointed other teams at their school have not initiated their own whole learning programs.

Sadly, most teachers and parents still think of the curriculum as a written "curriculum guide," a textbook, or a test, so the idea of inventing their own curriculum is daunting to say the least. If curriculum is not treated as both process and content, it continues to be regarded as set in time, rather than everchanging to adapt to new ideas and needs.

Here we go beyond the concept of curriculum as a fixed point to suggest the idea of curriculum as a series of points on a continuum. Some points on this continuum are more responsive to the needs of young adolescents while other points are more comfortable for teachers. Although, the purpose of the continuum is to give points of reference, we can't neglect the data and experiences of teachers and students which point clearly to curriculum integration as the way to developmental responsiveness.

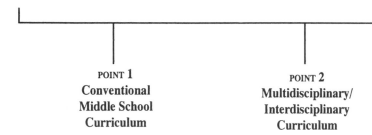

POINT 1
Conventional
Middle School
Curriculum

POINT 2
Multidisciplinary/
Interdisciplinary
Curriculum

Curriculum development must be seen as a more fluid process whereby we move along a scale. As we learn more about student need and as we confront our own values and beliefs about learning, we develop more skills in planning and implementing curriculum at increasingly more sophisticated levels.

The curriculum continuum outlined above gives teachers a framework for investigating where they currently are, the implications for being at that particular point, and the implications for themselves and their students in moving up and down the scale.

The curriculum continuum

The apparent mismatch between what we know the curriculum could and should be compared to what it usually is in middle level schools must be eliminated. The curriculum continuum provides a framework to visualize the possibilities of the middle level curriculum, organization, and content. It allows one to see the advantages and disadvantages for students and teachers as well as the characteristics of various types of curricula. Most importantly, we believe that the descriptions of the process of moving from point to point on the continuum, will be of real assistance in making desired changes. The purpose of the descriptions for each of the points on the continuum is to allow readers to see where they currently are, where they would like to be, and how they might get there.

The curriculum continuum offers a developmental look at curriculum which should be understandable to all who know young adolescents. Some positions are better and more appropriate for students, while some are more comfortable and less threatening for teachers. And yet many teachers recognize that their comfort should not be a factor in failing to change something that isn't best for young adolescents, in this case, the curriculum.

While the number of points on the continuum are limitless, we describe five key points each representing a major curriculum stance, giving a description of the curriculum characteristics, the role of students, and the role of teachers for each point.

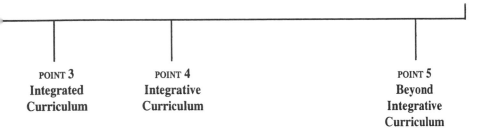

POINT 3
Integrated
Curriculum

POINT 4
Integrative
Curriculum

POINT 5
Beyond
Integrative
Curriculum

Conventional middle school curriculum

At the far left on the continuum (Point 1) is the conventional curriculum which exists in most middle schools today. This curriculum is characterized by all of the regularities with which we are familiar—a separate subject approach, textbook as the primary source of information, teacher in charge of everything, planning, teaching, evaluating. There is little or no student involvement or input into any aspect of the teaching-learning process. In fact, there is little analysis of learning, because the emphasis is on what the teacher does—teaching—not on what students do. Students spend much of their time in classes taking notes on teacher presented information, answering questions about readings from a textbook, or completing worksheets from accompanying workbooks. Success is measured in quantifiable terms, standardized and unit tests, course completion, and amount of time spent in class.

Students in this curriculum have some, but very limited choices of learning activities or experiences. School is still organized by subjects and students are given few opportunities to self-select among activities; likewise, they see few connections between and among the various courses. Curriculum is set by school and state guidelines, with assistance from textbook authors, and other "expert" groups.

The conventional school curriculum is based on the underlying assumption that if teachers, who should know best what students need, "build" an appropriate curriculum, then students will respond to it. It doesn't take too long by looking at conventional curriculum in most schools to see that for many students that has not been and is still not the case. Stanley Pogrow (1993), illustrates a variation on this theme; he thought that if students were prepared for rigorous work then appropriate coursework would be available to them. "I had assumed that if I could deliver students who were ready for rigorous coursework, the system could deliver it" (p. 42). For too many students the system couldn't and still doesn't deliver.

The conventional curriculum is college-like: students are often passive, and are expected to learn what the teacher presents with little attempt to place skills, knowledge and attitudes in a situation where they might be used. Here learning for the sake of learning ignores application.

Yet, even in schools like those represented by Point 1, some attempts at interdisciplinary work occur in separate, isolated classrooms. For example, an English teacher realizing that literature and writing is more effective if taught through the use of a unifying theme, rather than separate skills, formulates a unit which does just that. While little or no cross-subject integration occurs, individual teachers may experiment with interdisciplinary connections within their own subject(s) and in their own classes. Students may thus have an opportunity to pursue a project which is related to a theme under study.

Curiously, in spite of a number of signs which indicate that conventional curriculum does not meet the needs of young adolescents, most schools continue to rely heavily on it. It is, in fact, the "norm" in most schools across the U.S. In the series of shadow studies conducted by John Lounsbury and colleagues, the authors note that although many middle level schools are pleasant places for young adolescents, they are boring and students are not actively engaged in their own learning (1980, 1988, 1990).

Multidisciplinary curriculum

Point 2 represents the curriculum which many middle level schools *THINK* they must have to be a "true" middle school. As such it represents a move from a totally separate subject approach (Point 1) to some beginnings of what is generally referred to as "interdisciplinary" work; in actuality, it is closer to multidisciplinary, where several teachers from the same team offer work related to a central theme or topic, but in their own separate subject classrooms. A multidisciplinary unit on survival would focus on various aspects of survival—physical, psychological, and social—studied separately in various classes. In language arts, for example, students might read *Alive* or *Robinson Crusoe*, while in social studies, students might study survivors in a historical context, the Donner Party, the Lewis and Clark Expedition, and others. Not all subjects devote equal time to the multidisciplinary topic, but contribute when they can. These units often pique previously untapped student interests, because teachers have chosen a topic they are interested in and that enthusiasm is reflected in the enthusiasm that characterizes their teaching.

Responding to the current interest in curriculum, with its emphasis on making connections across the disciplines, as well as the need by some schools to advance the excellent work they have done in other areas to curriculum, many schools try out a variety of activities to make their curriculum more multidisciplinary, so Point 2 can represent a broad range of activities.

These activities take many forms, for example, a single day Renaissance festival, a week-long celebration of selected foreign countries, a longer multidisciplinary unit on the Rain Forest. Activities might range from a simple correlation of subjects to the beginnings of integrated units where subject boundaries are blurred. For example, a block of time may be devoted to studying a problem or issue such as "How will the environment survive?"

As diverse as they are in representing various types of multidisciplinary curriculum, the one characteristic these activities have in common is that they exist OUTSIDE the "regular" curriculum. As interesting, exciting, fun, and thought-provoking as these projects may be, ultimately, they are not regarded as the serious business of school. The separate subject approach is clearly the driving force of the school even though more and more teachers and students can attest to the value, both intellectual and social, which multidisciplinary studies promote.

These activities are merely a break-in-the-action and because they are regarded as such, do not take their full place of importance in the regular curriculum. These types of beginning interdisciplinary/integrated studies can be both beneficial and harmful. The successful activities of such a unit are not given their due, regarded as too much fun, while the unsuccessful often serve to reinforce the negative stereotype of integrated learning— "it takes too much time," "it is too fragmented," " it ignores central and important information," " it is not presented systematically," and many others. Nevertheless, as a beginning step, multidisciplinary units may serve to "open" the curriculum toward further curriculum integration.

The integrated curriculum

The next point (3) on the curriculum continuum builds on successful work with multidisciplinary units and leads to even more serious questioning and study of curriculum issues and processes. High levels of student learning, motivation, and interest in multidisciplinary and interdisciplinary projects, usually occurring in separate subject classrooms, encourage teachers to consider the next logical move—blurring lines between subjects.

By dissolving subject boundaries and using a block of time approach, students can pursue topics and themes across subject lines. Math, science, social studies, language arts and other areas identified as critical content, skills, and attitudes are studied within the context of such a unit. For example, a unit of study on rainforests might include reading a variety of nonfiction material about rainforests, studying the controversy about the reported disappearance of the rainforests, investigating the ecology of rainforests, making predictions about their survival, and mapping the geography and topography of rainforest regions.

Recognizing the importance of moving beyond the arbitrary and often artificial boundaries of subjects, integrated curriculum allows the learner to study a theme or topic by using content, skills, and concepts formerly reserved for particular subjects. What does this look like in schools? Most noticeable, perhaps, is that students do not move from subject to subject every 45 minutes. In a classroom where curriculum is integrated, there is a more seamless flow to the day. Large blocks of time are available for students to pursue topics, develop skills, and work in various groups on activities which involve serious consideration. As in the real world, when serious work needs to be done, persons become engaged in learning because they see that they are doing something that has meaning to them.

The distance between multidisciplinary and integrated curricula (points 2 and 3 on the continuum) is considerable, for it requires teachers to make a fundamental shift in their thinking about how and what students should learn. Because of this challenge, some teams never move beyond an occasional multidisciplinary unit while other teams, students, and schools consciously move to integrated learning as they recognize the limitations of the separate subject approach. Concerned about taking that bigger step to integration, schools at this point often maintain some level of the conventional curriculum and schedule. The danger is that doing both—integrated curriculum and conventional curriculum—will prevent maximum use of resources, particularly human resources, and the frustration of trying to run both systems may cause the new approach to break down.

At this point on the continuum, more and more time is devoted to integrated projects. For the first time, integration is regarded as critical, not merely tangential to learning. Occasionally, not far below the surface remains the nagging doubt that too much of the conventional curriculum will be lost by devoting time to integrated themes and we are "giving up time for covering the regular curriculum."

But the prime issue is attitudinal, not mechanical. Do we trust our own collective instincts—teachers, students, parents—as John Arnold (1985) wrote nearly 10 years ago in describing the "responsive curriculum," Do we trust our collective instincts to do what we know needs to be taught, in the way that it needs to be taught?

"When are skills taught?" "Isn't there some content that all should know?" These are two of the classic questions of concerned teachers who think that many aspects of the traditional curriculum are lost with curriculum integration. Not true! As with any other type of curriculum, teachers must decide (and must know) what students should learn before they begin this process. The role of students, less passive than in other types of curriculum processes, has as a key feature, opportunities to choose from a variety of teacher-planned activities. For as we have seen, a problem with curricula represented by points 1 and 2 on the continuum occurs when students spend so much time answering questions of others, instead of posing their own questions.

Examples of integrated curriculum exist in schools successful with multidisciplinary approaches and desirous of building on student interest and motivation. Some schools retain separate subject classes in the morning and allow students to work on integrated projects in the afternoon. Others allow classes or teams to pursue serious application work in an integrated fashion for one or two weeks at the conclusion of a unit. In both instances, such work is serious business, and regarded as such by both students and teachers.

The integrative curriculum

Classrooms using integrative and integrated curricula may look very much alike. But like an iceberg, two-thirds of their differences lie beneath the surface, subtle and less easily seen.

The prime feature of integrative curriculum (point 4) which distinguishes it from multidisciplinary (point 2) and integrated curricula (point 3) is the process of choosing topics of study, as well as who chooses. As exciting as multidisciplinary and integrated curricula often turn out to be for young adolescents, their fundamental flaw is that they are teacher-conceived and teacher-directed. Certainly students have options of choosing activities within the unit, but teachers choose the topic, activities, and methods of assessment. In comparison with conventional curriculum where students have few choices and where study of content and skills is divorced from application, multidisciplinary and integrated curriculum is quite exciting. But it doesn't go quite far enough. It doesn't involve students fully. It doesn't enlist their excitement for learning, their expertise, or their ingrained interest in learning.

As exciting as multidisciplinary and integrated curricula often turn out to be, their fundamental flaw is that they are teacher-conceived and directed.

In integrative curriculum where there is no artificial division of knowledge into separate subjects, students are the prime curriculum developers as they answer questions which reveal what is most important to them, what issues of the larger world are of interest to them, as well as those topics and issues which are important but are not included in their questions (McDonough, 1991).

Integrative middle level curriculum (point 4) goes well beyond the subject-centered teaching of the conventional curriculum; the obligatory pre-holiday unit on Pilgrims, mountains or kites in the multidisciplinary curriculum, and the blurring of subject lines in the integrated curriculum. Integrative curriculum

Subject matter is not discarded; it is re-positioned in a new form.

focuses on finding the answers to authentic questions of young adolescents, not as an add-on to the "regular" curriculum, but rather as THE curriculum. Subject matter is not discarded; it is re-positioned in a new form. Skills, content and behaviors are identified at the local level by teachers, students, their parents, and even administrators. Skills, content, and behaviors are selected because they are critical for young adolescents to know, to have, and be able to do. Curriculum emanates from continuing conversations about "what is most important to know." And from whom? The curriculum is organized into broad-based themes which students identify using a structured process. These themes then become the focus for all learning in which students engage. While they continue to work with teachers and other students in traditional ways, they also learn to work both in small groups and by themselves on a variety of learning activities.

But don't be misled by this description of the process. Before students pose questions which lead to selecting a theme of study, teachers must first determine their own expectations for the curriculum. Given the limited amount of time in a school day, what parameters exist for the middle level curriculum? This is where the difficult work comes in, because until now, teachers rarely have been asked or given the opportunity to investigate what the middle level curriculum should be.

Teachers do not abdicate their duties in an integrative curriculum, but rather work with students on a more equal basis. Often referred to as facilitators, teachers now are able to devote their time to teaching—assisting students in gaining understanding, tutoring, and monitoring progress rather than "instructing" a whole class.

Beyond integrative curriculum

Point 5 on the curriculum continuum is rarely seen in schools today on any sustained basis because it places huge responsibilities on students to recognize, plan, carry out, and evaluate what they want and need to learn. Many schools have some provision for independent or self-directed study, but few allow students to study in an area of interest for sustained periods. A good example of this point is to imagine the work in a museum, law office, or research laboratory. The purposeful, industrious, and focused way in which curators, attorneys, and scientists complete their work is an excellent model for student work. Largely self-directed, students pursue their own studies based on self interest or needs of that particular classroom or school.

The "beyond the integrative curriculum" is yet to be envisioned or articulated, but will most likely develop from students successful with integrative curriculum. These students will "demand" opportunities to study independently and at their own pace and will likely use technology to access great amounts of data, interact with a variety of sources, move out of the school site into the community and beyond, and participate in service projects, internships and "real" on-site work. Teacher and student roles will be partially reversed, or perhaps, intertwined, and students will have much more responsibility for setting direction for their own learning.

How to use the continuum

The points on the curriculum continuum are descriptive of ranges of possibilities in curriculum development. The process of moving from one point to another is not necessarily linear. For some, the process may be developmental, moving through multidisciplinary to integrated to integrative, but others may move directly to integrated or integrative as their skills and knowledge allow.

In reality, teams may be at several different points on the continuum at the same time. For example, Solon Elementary School (ME) teaches math in a conventional manner the first period of the day in separate classes, while the rest of the day is organized using an integrative curriculum. Other schools maintain "regular" classes in the morning and have a large block of time in the afternoon for either integrated or integrative curriculum. Still other schools, have a conventional curriculum for the better part of the year, interspersed with occasional interdisciplinary or multidisciplinary units.

Conclusion

Middle level curriculum development should focus on curriculum which is truly responsive to young adolescents' needs. Teachers must begin by asking such questions as, "how do we decide what is most important for young adolescents to know and be able to do" and "how do we integrate knowledge and skills?"

Teachers may be committed to curriculum integration conceptually, yet lack the knowledge and skill to fully implement it into their own classrooms. Teachers' commitment to curriculum integration comes with the realization that the conventional curriculum does not meet the needs of young adolescents, either in the content it provides, the skills it teaches, or most importantly, in the way it engages and involves students in their own learning.

A look ahead

In the next seven chapters real and exciting curriculum stories are told about individual schools or teams that were dissatisfied with the curriculum status quo in their schools; each school was a "successful" middle level school, doing many of the things which middle level schools do, but they also knew that there must be a more responsive curriculum for young adolescents and they wanted to find it.

These stories represent middle level schools from Kansas to Maine to Florida, and include single teachers, as well as teams of various sizes who have responded to "the next step." Each of these schools shared one goal, to make learning more relevant and meaningful for their students. How each school met this challenge is very different, as you will see, but each represents a significant attempt at integrating the curriculum.

Each of these stories holds a unique point on the curriculum continuum, and each is moving *away from* the separate subject approach. While placing these seven examples on the continuum is more than somewhat subjective, the continuum gives us a way to visualize the possibilities of a range of curricular responses. →

NOTE: In slightly altered form, this chapter appeared in *The New England League of Middle Schools Journal,* Spring 1994, and in the subsequent publication *Second Generation Curriculum—What and How We Teach at the Middle Level,* by Brazee and Capelluti, NELMS, 1994.

II

STORIES OF SUCCESS IN CURRICULUM INTEGRATION

Truth always originates in a minority of one, and
every custom begins as a broken precedent.
—Will Durant

To seek and to find a method by which teachers teach
less and learners learn more.
—John Amos Comenius, 1650

4

INTEGRATED STUDIES
FOR MULTI-AGE CLASSROOMS

Mary Bilodeau-Callan and Judith Bossie

Solon Elementary School began with the common elements of middle school, then moved on to curriculum integration as its unifying theme, realizing that lasting change will come only when the curriculum is improved. Savvy change agents, this team carefully documents their changes and outcomes.

Solon School is one of five K-8 buildings belonging to Maine School Administrative District #74 situated along the Kennebec and Carrabasset Rivers in central Maine. Two primary industries and a handful of small mills in the five communities make up the district. The largest mill employs nearly three hundred people. All of these businesses make wood products and most of the employees earn minimum wage or little more.

At Solon Elementary School, the primary team is made up of kindergarten through grade two. Grades one and two share students and classroom space. Together, these teachers plan and co-teach thematic units for their students throughout the year. Grades three and four have worked with the primary team planning and implementing several thematic units of study throughout the 1992-93 school year. During the 1993-94 school year, grade five joined these teachers as they began to implement thematic units and some multi-age components into their program.

Since 1989, the middle level team has included teachers and students in grades five through eight. For the past two years, these students have been combined into heterogeneous, multi-age groupings. Grade Five students start the year as a separate group, rotating among five teachers and continuing that pattern until students become accustomed to the teachers and their expectations; at that point they move onto multi-age teams.

Evolving curriculum design

Our Integrated Studies for Multi-age Classrooms Model (ISMAC) has evolved over the past six years as an outgrowth of James Beane's curriculum planning with students and teachers. We have implemented new teaching strategies and planned our program using what we have learned about the needs of middle level students, best practice, and learning styles. Our schedule and class syllabi are based on The Copernican Plan (Carroll, 1989). Six years ago we had a fifth grade teacher with a strong background in math and writing, sixth and eighth grade teachers whose strengths were in social studies, reading, and language arts, and a seventh grade teacher who had a strong science and math background; so we decided to become departmentalized using a junior high school organizational plan. Unfortunately, we had many students who were unsuccessful under this plan. To create a program to better meet the needs of the seventy-eight students in grades 5-8, we talked about and shared the highlights of what we had learned through coursework and professional readings. Changes began when we started talking together about our students and their needs.

Currently, we have a district curriculum guide that identifies the content and skills to be covered at each grade level. We use this document as a general guide to assure parents that all of the students in the district are being exposed to the same content and thus, are at the same "level of readiness" for high school.

When planning for thematic or topical units, we cross-check content and skills from the district curriculum guide that fit into the specific courses we develop. Students take two different, four week courses on some aspect of the theme. At the end of each four week block, students choose another pair of classes around the same theme. Most of the content and skills for the first unit "Health," were related to science, math, and health. In the "Trash to Cash" course, there are many opportunities to integrate language arts and math skills from the district curriculum. In "Bugs Under Glass" and "The Inside Story" we included specific content and skills from the science curriculum.

Using Beane's guidelines on student-teacher planning, we begin by having all students and staff members meet in mixed groups of 4-6. Generally, two teachers facilitate the process while all other adults, including educational technicians, participate with the students.

First, we have participants reflect on the questions and/or concerns they have about the world. After group members share their thoughts, a recorder from each group documents the questions and concerns that are shared by at least two people in the group. These are recorded on a chart in question form.

Next, we ask everyone to think of questions and/or concerns they have about themselves. The same process is repeated and the recorder again writes down shared questions on the chart.

We then ask the groups to read through their questions to find overlaps which become themes. For example, students often have many questions about how the world might end, how they might die, and if there is an afterlife. These topics are commonly grouped under the theme of "death and dying."

Once all groups have determined what their themes are, we ask them to share with the whole class. While one facilitator records the themes on a chart, the other asks clarifying questions so that participants hear what led up to the selection of each theme. This processing then leads the whole group to an understanding of the common questions and concerns shared by all involved.

Once all the possible themes from each group are shared and recorded, participants are led through a voting procedure to help narrow down the themes to five or six choices. From these themes, they select the top three they would like to investigate for the year. After the three themes are selected, participants quickly decide in what order they want to study them. Then we ask them to return to their original questions about themselves and the world to identify which ones could be answered through each theme. We also ask them to add any other questions they may have which they would like answered while studying each theme.

The final step in the process is for participants to generate activities which will help them to study the theme. We have found this to be extremely valuable as their suggestions for activities combined with their questions are the key elements of our planning for the courses and themes. Once we have the questions and activities, teachers meet and look for general "themes within the theme" that lend themselves to courses. For example, many students had questions about "why animals become endangered" so one of the courses in the Animal and the Environment theme focused specifically on this topic. In addition, teachers identify areas they would personally like to investigate and teach in those areas. Then they design the courses by identifying student outcomes, selecting the materials and resources, and developing methods of evaluation. The planning process just described is the key to the success of these units.

The planning process is the key to the success of these units.

Teachers identify two types of outcomes for each course, content and global. The content objectives describe the specific content that students are expected to learn in each course. We also identify skills and attitudes from Maine's Common Core of Learning that we expect students to successfully develop for each course. We call these the global outcomes.

In the process of developing our courses, we refer to the Individual Education Plans for those students with special needs. When necessary, we modify the coursework so that these students are able to meet the objectives for the course. Typical modifications for those who have a disability in written language include providing students with copies of notes and pages from resources on the topic of study.

Since students participate in these courses for four weeks, we have the opportunity to continually refine the courses as we re-teach them. Students frequently keep journals during the courses and we use their feedback, our own observations, and input from fellow teachers, administrators, and parents when making decisions about changing and improving the courses.

The culminating activities for each course vary according to the thematic unit. For the unit on Health, students spent one week developing a project that reflected what they had learned during the course of study. Examples included a student survey of the hot lunch program; a video tape of a visiting EMT explaining the equipment in an ambulance; a unit of study on CPR students taught to the lower grades in our school; and a comprehensive lesson on sexually transmitted diseases that students developed with the district school nurse. These were presented to the school board and taught to grades seven and eight in our school. The students demonstrated these and many other projects during a community open house at the end of the Health unit.

Another successful culminating activity was a personal newsletter written by each student. At the end of the unit on Communications, students were asked to choose five of the courses that they had taken and to write a commentary on each one, including what they liked and didn't like, what they would and would not change, and what they learned from each course. They also wrote a letter to the editor about some aspect of communication that they felt strongly about. Some students also included a political cartoon based on one of the courses studied, "Freedom of Speech...A Look at the Constitution and the Bill of Rights."

The Communications Newsletter also served as an evaluation for us as students expressed their opinions about the courses they had taken. Students also give us feedback on a regular basis through daily journal writing and quarterly surveys where they express their opinions about the specific courses as well as about multi-age groupings, the cooperative learning groups, and the amount of homework assigned. As a result of these surveys, we decided to rethink our homework policy. Some team members located recent research on homework at the middle level and shared their findings with the team. Team members are now much more thoughtful about assigning homework.

Another way we evaluate our program is to look at individual student performance. Are they meeting content and global outcomes that we expect them to? The overwhelming answer to that question at this time is "Yes." All but three percent of the students are successfully meeting at least 80 percent of the course objectives on a consistent basis. After each unit is completed, we talk as a team about what worked particularly well and what didn't. We also ask parents what they think of the courses and how their children are performing. One of the most common concerns from parents initially was that their son or daughter was doing "too well" in school. For many students, this was the first time that they had been given the opportunity to show what they know and to gain understandings through their own strengths and learning styles. We also use the results of district standardized tests and the Maine Educational Assessment results as indicators of student performance.

This was the first time many students had the opportunity to show what they know and to gain understandings through their own strengths and learning styles.

We are in the process of starting portfolios with our students. We have selected some pieces of work from this year for each student so that they will have the beginning of their portfolios for the fall. We have also planned a week at the end of each course when students will purposefully reflect on what they have learned during the theme and determine what evidence best illustrates this learning. These artifacts will then become part of their portfolios.

One final method of evaluation that we use is input from the various visitors to our school throughout the year. We have found that people from outside the school very often have a perspective on what is happening that is extremely helpful to us. We host visitors from throughout Maine and New England each Wednesday. Their observations and questions help us to be clearer about what we are doing and how we are meeting the needs of our students.

We realize that our approach to integrating the curriculum may seem idealistic to some. Remember, we didn't start where we are now, either!

Implementing the ISMAC model

During weekly planning time, team members meet and brainstorm specific courses related to the chosen theme. We share ideas about possible sources of information for the unit and we use the district curriculum as a guide in the specific content areas to be covered in the unit. For example, our district curriculum for grades six through eight includes the Skills for Adolescence Program (Quest), so we include units from this program within the larger unit.

Next, teachers plan individual courses they will teach by preparing syllabi, selecting content and global objectives, determining evaluation procedures, and developing a timeline for each course. Teachers also collect resources for themselves and their students and prepare daily lesson plans that correspond to the course objectives.

Once the unit is ready, team members discuss possibilities for scheduling the courses. We decide the order in which we will teach the courses and develop a rotation for them.

Students begin their day by attending two classes, one based on the theme, and a math class, each lasting 80 minutes. The courses run for four weeks and students choose the order in which they take them. After the first eight weeks of the unit, teachers rotate the order of the courses so that students have the chance to select from all, as well as offer students the opportunity to engage in more hands-on learning.

At the end of four weeks teachers send home a progress report designed by parents and teachers informing parents how their child has done in a course for the traditional quarterly report card. The report was designed by teachers and parents during the 1992-93 school year.

Data collection

Because the middle level program in Solon is unique for the district, we have been deliberate in collecting various types of data on our students and their learning. As previously described, we have systematically collected input from a student survey, at least twice a year.

A second form of data we collect has been particularly valuable to us in developing the ISMAC model. Each year we administer the Learning Styles Profile (Dunn, Dunn, Price, 1975, 1978) to the new group of fifth graders entering our program. We use the information from these profiles in a variety of ways. For example, we have discovered that fewer than five percent of our students prefer bright/direct lighting when they study. Because of this finding, we have removed most of the fluorescent lighting in our classrooms. Those few students who need bright light either sit directly beneath one of the remaining lights or next to a window. The information gathered from these inventories also allows us to determine the best way to structure the classroom environment and activities. We take time to share the inventories with individual students and parents. Most importantly, we teach our students about learning styles in general and assist individuals in developing strategies to compensate for weaknesses or to capitalize on strengths. Every two years we reassess students' learning styles and when new students enter our program we assess their styles as well.

A third source of data is course objectives. At the end of each course, teachers check off the objectives which students have successfully met. Over the span of the year, a profile on each student emerges. At mid-year, the team will look at the data on each student and determine what areas each student needs to concentrate on during the remainder of the year. It is our intent that all students will successfully meet each objective before leaving Solon and entering high school.

One very important part of our data collection is the feedback that students offer on specific courses. They are brutally honest, which helps us to refine our teaching strategies and classroom organization. For example, after students participated in a course in physical and mental health, they offered suggestions about how the course could be improved for the next group of students. A consistent recommendation from students was to schedule gym time less frequently, but for longer blocks of time so that they could have more time experimenting with various pieces of equipment. Much of this type of course evaluation surfaces in the daily journals kept by students as well as through teacher-designed course evaluation forms.

These data combined with standardized test results tell us that we have a very diverse group of students with diverse learning styles. Because of this diversity, it is essential that we continue to find ways to develop learning opportunities that are personally meaningful for each of our students. We must also find other ways to assess what our students truly know and are able to do.

> **It is essential that we continue to find ways to develop learning opportunities that are personally meaningful for each of our students.**

We are currently working on ways to incorporate alternative assessment. Each month, teachers and parents meet to discuss such topics as portfolios, authentic assessment, and standards. At this time, we are addressing mathematics and science. Traditionally, our students have performed very well in math on standardized measures. However, our recent readings of the NCTM standards has led us to question whether we are really preparing our students to apply math in meaningful ways.

Change is difficult

There have been obstacles to overcome during this process of change. A small group of parents has resisted our efforts to change the traditional pattern of organization and instruction. These parents would prefer to see their children sitting at desks, in rows, with an open textbook in front of them. Another problem has been insufficient funding for our program. State financial support to our district has decreased substantially in each of the past three years. This has burdened our program in two important areas: common planning time and itinerant scheduling. Currently, students are pulled out of academic classes for itinerant programs.

We have created team planning time in a variety of ways: several years ago we wrote a grant which provided funds to pay community members to teach exploratory classes. These one hour classes were taught twice each week, for five weeks. The grant also provided money to purchase materials for these classes. As this was only a one year grant, the following year we had to be creative by planning whole-group activities that were supervised by teachers as the team planned in the same room: a speaker, an educational video, silent reading, or small group projects. These activities were always tied to the unit and were used with pre and post activities. Currently, educational technicians "cover" our classrooms for 90 minutes each week so we can plan together. We also meet sometimes in the evening, on Saturdays, and during the summer. On five Wednesday afternoons during the year all students in the district are dismissed at noontime. Our team uses these half days for team planning, and on some of our seven workshop days, our team is excused from the district inservice activities for team planning.

To keep parents and the community informed about key elements of our program, articles from journals on current educational practices and research have been sent home with each student on a weekly or biweekly basis for the past four years. In addition, we have presented programs on middle level practices, learning styles, and cooperative learning to the school board and district PTO groups. We have held frequent parent meetings where we made presentations using cooperative learning structures. We have had many open houses to give parents and community members the opportunity to see student work at the end of an integrated studies unit. Finally, because we are well-read and up-to-date on current research, we have won the administrative support necessary to make our program possible. Through these efforts, we have many happy and supportive parents; however, there are still a few who do not see our program as one which will have their children ready for high school.

Indicators of success

Improved academic performance is a clear benefit of the program

Student academic performance is one strong benefit of this program. Those who were successful in the traditional classroom remain successful. Students with disabilities in written language who are mainstreamed, now refuse the assistance of an aide who is available to script for them. They choose to write out their own work instead. Students who have continuously underachieved in school now consistently achieve at 80 percent rate or better. Student journals and surveys point out the in-class activities and teaching strategies that have helped to bring successes to students who traditionally were at-risk. Students also have taken more responsibility for their learning since they are able to choose from a menu of options in order to meet class objectives. The more success they have realized, the higher their self-esteem has grown. High self-esteem and academic success feed from one another.

Students are making connections. This is evident in their writing and in class discussions. Students used to ask if they could use material learned in one class to support an idea they were working on in another class, but now they have grown beyond the idea that this is "cheating" and have come to accept the fact that once they have learned something, it belongs to them. In some cases, because we do not use discipline labels (language arts, science and others), students are unable to recognize which class they are in!

Student behavior has improved greatly, both in class and on the playground.

Student behavior has improved greatly, both in class and on the playground. Students are truly engaged in their learning; whether they are taking notes or working cooperatively on a group activity, they understand the purpose of what they are doing. Harmony on the playground may be attributed to grouping in the classroom. Students are constantly with different groups as they travel from class to class and are assigned to cooperative learning groups within each class. This has enabled them to learn to get along with everyone. Small cliques have broken up and former isolates are now found enjoying an activity on the playground with newfound friends. A recent survey of our students showed 41% of them identified positive attitudes towards others as an essential attitude for them to have.

Another success is the improvement of communication among staff. All important decisions are made through consensus, whether in planning for curriculum or problem-solving. We rarely agree on a solution at the start, but we talk it through and always come to consensus for a plan of action. If plan A fails, we meet in the hall at recess, before and/or after school; then we implement plan B. Our classroom doors are always open. We share materials and help one another: we have all learned the true meaning of flexibility and collaboration.

The final success we share is increased community involvement at our school. Our open invitation to unannounced visits has proven beneficial in two ways. First, we ask all visitors to complete a questionnaire before they leave; thus giving us insightful information, and helping visitors think about the purposes and outcomes of activities they have observed. Second, the PTO furnishes much of the necessary funding to purchase current resource materials needed in our creative courses.

Parents assist students in the classrooms, and several assist staff with secretarial duties and in athletic programs. All who spend time in the school see the results of our efforts and spread the news to parents who either are not able to be in the classroom or feel ill-at-ease in the school setting.

More team planning time is needed for trouble-shooting sessions in order to have plans B and C ready in the event that plan A should fail. One example of trouble-shooting addressed the method in which we were sending the course syllabi home to parents. We started by sending them home with the students during the first week of classes. However, given young adolescents' proclivity for losing or forgetting materials that don't appear important to them, we now send home the syllabi for all courses in an envelope that is signed by the parents and returned (empty) to the school before the unit begins. This gives parents an opportunity to help students select courses and it also gives parents a clear description of the rationale, student expectations, and course content in advance. This has eliminated much of the time we spend explaining the program to a series of individual parents during the first week of each new unit. More team planning time would permit us to address problems, such as the one described, much more quickly and efficiently.

Evaluation of our work

There are several means through which we have gained parent and community involvement. We informally "try out" ideas on parents when we meet with them individually in a casual setting. We target those who generally have concerns, those who are vocal, and those who are respected by the community. We also enlist community members with special interests and talents who enhance our program. We use these valuable resource people in our planning, on field trips, or as guest speakers for our students. Many have talked about their occupations, exhibited collections, or taught "how to" classes.

Additionally, there is a need to have parents involved with the team in our formal planning process. We have studied alternative forms of assessment for several years —attending workshops and reading everything available on the topic. We continue to work with a group of parents on this topic.

Evaluation after the completion of our first thematic unit was insightful. First, we agreed that individual project time should have been more structured. We now offer a menu of topics and activities from which students may choose. Students are becoming more comfortable in using their creativity within each unit, and we find ourselves stamping approval on more and more outlines of innovative projects now. We feel that this student ability is an outcome of the structure and guidelines that we have provided for them.

Second, we have learned the value of keeping the total school staff informed. Individual members of the staff are questioned by community members every day. It is vital that they are well-informed and that they give accurate information.

Third, we learned that many of the pitfalls might have been avoided with frequent and consistent common planning time. We are still using our creativity to provide the time necessary to meet. For example, one solution to provide planning time for our team has come through a grant to pay members to participate in four, day-long planning sessions throughout the summer.

A final lesson we have learned is that change is not accepted by all and that a few parents remain concerned about the changes we have implemented. Much time has been spent with these parents in order that they be given the opportunity to voice their specific concerns and to find solutions for them whenever possible. It is not always possible to satisfy every concern. In some cases the requests have not been consistent with best practice and/or meeting the needs of young adolescents. In other cases minor modifications have led to compromises between parents and the team. Ultimately, some parents have opted to send their children to other more traditional schools in the district.

In summary, we believe that there are six key elements that must be considered before undertaking the ISMAC Model or any similar model.

- **Know current research and professional literature.**
- **Involve parents from the beginning and throughout the process of change.**
- **Keep everyone informed at all times. Parents, staff, school board members, administrators, and key community persons comprise a *must* list for continuing communication.**
- **Be prepared for conflict and resistance and be prepared to meet it with a willingness to collaborate and compromise.**
- **Win the support of administrators and school board members as quickly as possible.**
- **Be flexible. Change is not permanent. It is ongoing with constant modifications as needs surface.**

While this work has not been easy, the benefits for students, parents, teachers, and ultimately the community, have been well worth the efforts. →

5   HAND-CRAFTING AN INTEGRATED CURRICULUM

Laura Boutilier

Timothy Edwards Middle School in South Windsor, Connecticut, has used a number of curriculum models as it attempts to meet the needs of young adolescents. Encouraged to take risks, the staff has provided a variety of developmentally responsive curriculum practices for its students. Assessment data indicate their efforts have been productive.

A truly integrated curriculum is much like a hand-crafted patchwork quilt. Each piece of the design fits together with other pieces to make a complete pattern. The individual pieces can be as diverse as the colors in a rainbow or shapes in the geometric world. Yet all pieces are joined together with a common thread that binds and helps create a finished piece of work.

The designs or blocks that make up a quilt are representative of the various disciplines that comprise a curriculum. Each has its own shape and content. Each is unique in what it brings to the child's educational experience. Each combines with others to form a comprehensive whole.

Student outcomes are the common thread that unify this curriculum. At Timothy Edwards Middle School we have developed numerous "quilts" as we have integrated our curriculum in a variety of ways and for a variety of purposes.

The background pieces

Nestled among apple orchards in South Windsor, Connecticut, lies Timothy Edwards Middle School. The town, a suburb of Hartford, is located approximately eleven miles to the east of the capital city. Many of the natives still perceive their town as the old tobacco farming community that it once was. As a matter of fact, many tobacco farms coexist today with booming businesses and industry. However, much open land and a close proximity to Hartford has created a fast-growing community. The resulting increase in population has created challenges for the education system as we accommodate expanded enrollments. Presently the town's population is approximately 22,000 citizens repre-

51

senting a fairly upwardly mobile population. Within this town, there are four elementary schools, one comprehensive high school and one middle school. Timothy Edwards Middle School is a 920 student school that adopted a middle school philosophy nine years ago. First time visitors to the school are greeted with a banner proclaiming "We Bring Good Kids Through Life." This motto is one we believe in and live everyday. As middle school educators, we recognize the responsibility we have been charged with—to be responsive to each individual child during a transitional period in his or her life. Our student population is divided among nine interdisciplinary teams of teachers who strive to meet the unique needs of our young adolescents.

The process of creating a quilt

In 1983, the staff at Timothy Edwards, then organized as a junior high school, completed a comprehensive study of middle school philosophy, programs and practices. Various committees were charged with moving a 7-9 junior high school to a 6-8 middle school. Study committees worked over an entire year, visiting other schools, conducting research, and reaching consensus as to what their middle school would look like. The school made the commitment to adopt a middle school philosophy and implement a team arrangement, flexible scheduling, and extensive exploratory programs. At that time, no thought was given to curricular changes except as they related to the amount of time students spent receiving direct instruction in each subject area.

The curriculum followed a traditional model with emphasis on developing basic skills in math, language arts, science, and social studies, as it had before conversion to a middle school. Added exploratory courses included music, foreign language, physical education, and unified arts (art, home economics, and industrial arts). Since that time, industrial arts has evolved into a technology education program, computer education has been added, and foreign language has become a mandatory course for all seventh and eighth graders.

Following this organizational change, content area teachers continued to teach their disciplines in isolation from each other. The need for coordination and leadership was met by creating the positions of team leaders and a school-wide curriculum coordinator for each discipline. Professional development activities for staff focused on becoming more effective in implementing middle school philosophy and practices.

Each interdisciplinary team of teachers consisted of a math, science, English, social studies, and foreign language or reading teacher who met daily to discuss students and student issues. They coordinated expectations, calendars, tests, and homework, and they met regularly with students, parents, guidance counselors, and administrators. They provided collegial support for each other as they shared frustrations and successes in working with middle school age youngsters.

Teachers provided collegial support for each other sharing frustrations and successes.

With most of the other middle school practices firmly in place, emphasis shifted to interdisciplinary instruction. Although the original job description developed for team leaders required "an interdisciplinary unit to be developed each year," the coordination of the curriculum was not given much emphasis. For the first time, teams were required to "try out an interdisciplinary unit." They were given the option of developing a day-long unit or a more extensive project. They were asked to take a risk with much support provided. Guidelines were given, past successes were shared, and resources were made available.

During all of this time teachers regularly attended The New England League of Middle School Conference and other locally sponsored conferences and workshops. Their enthusiasm and project ideas were shared with colleagues. In fact, all nine teams developed an interdisciplinary unit that year.

From this early dialogue about curriculum, a sixth grade Family History Day resulted. This month-long genealogy project integrates instruction in English, math, science, social studies, music, and art classes. A family tree as well as a written family history is created by each student. A day long Family History Celebration attended by some 500 grandparents, parents, and children in 1993 culminated this extensive interdisciplinary unit. One parent, Joseph J. Kristan, Jr., made this assessment:

> I left Timothy Edwards School after lunch with a profound sense of having been bound firmly, not only to the past, but also to the other families who participated in the program. I felt a renewed and strengthened pride in those who have gone before us, a clearer understanding of our place in the present and a less mysterious view of our future. The project was a time-out from our hurried and harried day-to-day concerns to reflect and remember. It provided me with an extraordinary perspective on the meaning and values of my family and the larger community. It was a privilege to participate in the Family History project and I owe a debt of thanks to all of the talented and dedicated teachers who worked very hard to make it all happen.

His sentiments were echoed by many who attended this extraordinary culminating activity. (This project is outlined later in this chapter.)

An eighth grade team coordinated the study of American history with a discussion of the novel *April Morning.* Home economics and art classes also became involved in this unit and it resulted in the development of a Thanksgiving Feast.

As you can see from these two examples, a variety of "quilts" were created by staff as a result of the emphasis placed on curricular changes. Many of these projects are still in place four years later and have been refined and embellished.

As a part of the original design for our middle school, the individual combinations of teachers on a team are changed every three years. Team members are reshuffled to encourage change in the collaborative groups. With this change comes the sharing of project ideas, curricular overlaps, and teaching methodology. This policy has facilitated the exchange of many good ideas between team members, teachers at other grade levels, and in other subject areas. Collaboration is emphasized and integration is the natural result.

Having come as far as we could with making connections while still maintaining our separate disciplines, it was apparent that a formal workshop on planning for an integrated curriculum was needed. Although many staff members had been to conferences and workshops, not all had been exposed to the same terminology or same concepts. There was an increasing need to talk the same language and share the same understandings.

Hearing from a classroom teacher helped many staff members understand the value and process of interdisciplinary instruction.

Sam Lewbel, a middle school colleague from the southern part of our state, spent a full day with our staff sharing his work in the development of interdisciplinary instruction. A step-by-step process for the development of an interdisciplinary unit was given and specific interdisciplinary unit projects from his school were also shared. Hearing from a classroom teacher helped many staff members understand the value and process of interdisciplinary instruction.

Weaving in the special areas

Although many attempts were made to involve the special areas (art, music, home economics, physical education, and technology education) in developing these units, schedules of these specialists did not always permit regular meeting times. The opportunity to collaborate with team teachers was difficult as meeting times were scheduled while students were receiving instruction in special area classes. Four years later this remains a major concern. Presently, we are exploring other options such as assigning special area teachers to teams or creatively working with the schedule to facilitate interdisciplinary instruction across all areas of the curriculum.

In spite of these obstacles, special area staff have done a commendable job of integrating subject matter. For instance, the physical education staff developed a school-wide Olympic Game Unit. In addition to involving the entire 700 student body in this integrated project, a message concerning the unique learning experiences all the special areas bring to the curriculum had ramifications that extended well beyond this project.

Sharing expertise and skill

As so often happens the most valuable lessons result from dialogue with colleagues. The New England League of Middle Schools Conference has spawned a number of innovations among our staff. Knowledge of an island field trip in a neighboring state, conducted with students in a gifted and talented program caught the attention of one of our attendees at the conference. This teacher shared his excitement with his team of four other eighth grade teachers. They then took the original ideas and adapted them to meet the needs of their team of ninety students. A two day interdisciplinary bike trip evolved from this collaboration. It since has become an integral part of our eighth grade end-of-the-year activities. As a matter of fact, some parents request this particular team assignment for their child because of this field trip opportunity.

A year later another eighth grade team adapted this original idea to a study on Martha's Vineyard in Massachusetts. They used professional development funds for an overnight trip for their four member team to travel to Martha's Vineyard. The time was spent traveling to the site, conducting their research, and developing a two day field trip which incorporated content from all four subject areas in a fun and challenging format. In addition to the development of a valuable learning activity, the time spent away from school conducting research in the appropriate setting has produced benefits that extend beyond this project. A successful two day overnight field trip resulted, but also the team bonding that occurred has had positive spin-offs even three years later. A participant, Paul Bernier, remarked, "This was one of the most rewarding experiences for me as a teacher. In addition to the relationships that were built with new team members, being treated as a professional created excitement and motivated us to create a unique experience for kids."

Moving on to the next step

Since all teams had become involved in interdisciplinary instruction to some degree, the staff seemed ready to progress to a higher level of involvement. At the start of the next school year, a local educator with expertise in thinking skills instruction was hired to work with the entire staff. The rationale was twofold. This topic was relevant to all middle level educators and therefore useful in any discipline. Also, this was a topic that most staff members had not been exposed to in their teacher training programs. An additional goal was to provide a less threatening way to become involved in interdisciplinary instruction for the reluctant teacher without compromising his/her content area by incorporating improved questioning strategies. Many aspects of thinking skills have since been included in the interdisciplinary units we have developed.

During the summer of 1991, Laura Boutilier, principal, attended a workshop with Robin Fogarty, a consultant in curriculum integration. Seeing the connection between Fogarty's ten models for integrating the curriculum and the direction Edwards Middle School was going, Boutelier adapted Fogarty's work, personalized it into a two hour long workshop, and presented it to the Edwards staff on the first day of school the following September. A critical part of the workshop was building in planning time for groups of teachers representing all disciplines to meet and develop their ideas on how best to deliver instruction in an integrated manner. The integration continuum she shared matched the diverse approaches the nine teams at Edwards used. As Fran Maynard, seventh grade teacher said, "The process of creating from a grass roots effort was as important as the end product." Among other projects that resulted was a highly successful unit, "Around the World in 180 Days," presently being used with the entire seventh grade class.

Ongoing support

Throughout these five years, time has been set aside at both team leader and curriculum coordinator meetings (each held bi-monthly) for sharing ideas, successes, and obstacles in integrating the curriculum. This sharing process has been both formal and informal. In order to encourage discussion among teachers on a particular grade level, a schedule has been designed so that the three teams of teachers on each grade level are allotted time once a month to meet and collaborate. For example, all twelve seventh grade teachers have built in planning time to work on their unit. At other times of the month, teachers meet by grade level and discipline in place of a team planing period. For example, all sixth grade math teachers have time set aside for them to meet and discuss curricular issues. At the same time all three sixth grade science teachers meet to discuss their subject area. There is no lack of expertise or enthusiasm among this very dedicated staff. Experience has shown that professionals grow when given time to collaborate. Fran Maynard, seventh grade teacher, shared this insight, "As a unit emerges and converges, we are not only making connections for our students but also for ourselves."

Experience has shown that professionals grow when given time to collaborate.

We had found that in spite of the best intentions, too many house-keeping and business items ended up taking very valuable team planning time that could have been spent on curricular discussion. Therefore, we have allocated one day per week to be held "sacred" for a discussion of curriculum. Wednesdays are designated "Curriculum Day." No guidance counselor, administrator, or social worker may plan parent meetings or other discussions with the teams on that day. Curriculum discussions are a vital and regular part of team plans.

One day per week is held "sacred" for a discussion of curriculum.

Joining the special area pieces

In addition to playing an integral role in the large scale interdisciplinary projects, many of the special area staff have worked very hard in the last few years to redefine their curriculum so that their curricular goals can be met while integrating with other subject areas. For example, the art staff has realigned the curriculum so that all of their projects intended to develop skills in the arts are taught within the context of a specific topic or unit from other subject areas. In completing a sixth grade clay project the art teachers instructed students to develop their clay figures in conjunction with their family history project mentioned above. Their character now might be dressed as an ancestor may have been.

In another instance, a resource person was brought in to facilitate the making of clay bowls using Japanese brush painting techniques which coordinated with the social studies unit on Japan. Likewise, home economics, technology education, and music staff have adapted their lessons to better coordinate with other subject areas. Cynthia Wallace-Bernier, art teacher, speaks for her entire department when she says, "It is still important to maintain the integrity of our own curriculum as a viable subject area while drawing connections among other content areas."

In addition to integrating with other subject areas, the unified arts teams (consisting of home economics, technology education and art teachers) have developed their own Sailboat Regatta. Students in sixth grade (over the course of the year spent in unified arts instruction) construct a catamaran type wooden sailboat in technology education classes, construct a sail for this boat in home economics classes, and then design and stencil this sail in their art classes. This project is then the focus of a sixth grade Sailboat Regatta held every spring on the school grounds. In order to embellish the Regatta Day activities, students in home economics classes plan games and activities, utilizing the skills they have learned in child development classes. In keeping with the sailboat theme, art students also compete in a sand sculpture design contest, using skills they have learned.

The connecting thread

As we have moved along the integration continuum throughout these eight years, it has become increasingly clear that there is a need to delineate what we expect our students to master at the end of their three year experience with us. To this end, curricular outcomes were developed. Each curriculum coordinator worked collaboratively with his or her department members to develop these outcomes. Initially four agreed upon strands were then woven into all curricular areas. The skills of *writing to learn, reading effectively, thinking critically,* and *learning to learn* appear throughout our program.

Presently we are in the process of sharing these outcomes with our parent community. Their feedback will be valuable information as we continually analyze and refine our expectations.

Parent and community involvement

Although parents and community members have not been directly involved in the planning of our interdisciplinary units, they are involved in the culminating activities of all of these units. We take advantage of these opportunities to facilitate communication between young adolescents and parents and parents and the school.

In some instances this may involve the child working closely with family members to make medieval costumes or conduct personal research into family histories. In other instances parent attendance at the culminating activities is a sign of their interest and support.

Student enthusiasm and interest in interdisciplinary projects has been extremely high.

This year our community police officer, who happens to teach our sixth grade DARE (Drug Abuse Resistance Education) program, will be designing and racing his own DARE boat as a part of the Regatta. He also will be bringing the DARE balloon and DARE car to add to the festivities for the day. Our collaboration with vital community members has benefits that extend beyond the particular project or activity.

Assessing our "quilts"

As one would expect, student enthusiasm and interest in interdisciplinary projects has been extremely high. Students are excited about this active involvement in their own learning. Sixth grader, Camille Malispina, summed up her experience with the Medieval Gala, "It was wicked fun!" Following every integrated unit teachers conduct assessments either using a portfolio approach or open ended questions. For example, following the two day Block Island trip students were asked a series of questions about their experiences. The results of these questions were then shared with the parents via the principal's newsletter so that they could see the growth that had occurred because of their child's involvement in this interdisciplinary field trip experience.

Next steps in the process of constructing "quilts"

At this stage in our evolution as a middle school, we are exploring other ways to more closely link curricular content among various disciplines. Next year we are hoping to assign special area teachers to each team on the sixth grade level. It is our hope that this will facilitate the valuable sharing that results in increased integration of subject matter. Some staff members are presently researching a totally thematic instructional approach similar to that advocated by James Beane.

With our curriculum outcomes formally in place, parental concerns about movement away from a traditional curricular delivery system should be minimized. Each individual teacher's movement along the integration continuum is guided by these outcomes. Flexibility exists for all professionals to reach these benchmarks without compromising their own teaching styles.

Integration of the curriculum is a process. Like hand-crafting a quilt, many diverse pieces must be brought together around a unifying theme. Like hand crafting a quilt, integration is a slow, thoughtful process. With any hand-crafted project, whether it be a quilt or a child's education, an element of caring is essential.

With any hand-crafted project, whether it be a quilt or a child's education, an element of caring is essential.

Throughout this story there has been an attempt to chronicle the nine year journey undertaken by Timothy Edwards Middle School as it has moved from a traditional junior high school to an integrated middle school. The journey is far from complete. However, during our travels we have grown as individuals as well as a school. →

6

ONE DISTRICT'S PERSPECTIVE: STAFF DEVELOP-
MENT STIMULATES CURRICULUM INTEGRATION

Sue Carol Thompson with Carol Stewart, Tonya Buckingham, Joann Hauser, and Karen Nelson

Blue Valley School District has five middle schools in this suburb of Kansas City. As a district that is devoted to responsive schools for young adolescents, programs have been provided that reflect that commitment. This story is the account of one team in one middle school that has made significant strides in working toward more curriculum integration.

Blue Valley School District, like many across the United States, decided to evaluate its middle level program and determine a future direction based on current research and literature about the most effective way to educate young adolescents. During the 1987-88 school year, a committee composed of teachers, parents, administrators, and board members met to study and share information about the characteristics and needs of young adolescents and the organizational structure needed to best meet those needs.

As a result of their findings, the Middle Level Study Committee Report recommended to the Board of Education five organizational changes to be implemented over a three-year period. The first of these changes was the implementation of interdisciplinary teaming, followed by a full range of exploratory classes, an expanded activity program, and an advisement program. The fifth component of the plan, staff development, has been ongoing over the past five years. The decision was also made to hire a middle level director who would oversee the new program. I was selected for that post based on sixteen years of experience as a middle school teacher, team leader, and principal.

At the same time, the district was developing new curriculum in the areas of language arts, science, mathematics, and social studies. Three new middle schools were built from 1988 through 1992, bringing the total of middle schools in the district to five. Even in the midst of much change, which occurred as some teachers moved from school to school every two years as new middle schools opened, several interdisciplinary teams cautiously began exploring ways to connect subject matter through multidisciplinary units. While these connections were definitely an improvement over the previous content fragmentation found in our middle schools, few teams had really bridged the gap from multidisciplinary to interdisciplinary teaching. Teachers remained subject specialists, teaching their subject several times over in 45 minute blocks of time.

My belief in the middle school philosophy for meeting the needs of each individual child was strong because of my previous experience as a core curriculum teacher in the early 70s and my own teaming experiences, which had been interdisciplinary in nature. After the completion of the three year implementation plan, the principals and I began exploring ways to make learning more meaningful and rich for our students under our new organizational structure.

In the fall of 1990, our administrators attended a workshop conducted by James Beane at the National Middle School Conference in Long Beach, California. His ideas on the integration of separate subject matter instruction through the use of questions students pose about themselves and their world made sense. We subsequently attended the NMSA Regional Conference in Minneapolis, Minnesota, in May 1991 that focused on restructuring the middle school curriculum. This conference was the starting point for our journey as a group of administrators into the issue of curriculum. It was a provocative topic that we debated and discussed intently as we closed the 1991 school year. We continued to explore the topic of curriculum integration by reading Beane's book, *The Middle School Curriculum: From Rhetoric to Reality* (1990a, 1993b). Numerous copies were handed out to interested teachers and study groups were established in some of the schools to give teachers a chance to share and respond to Beane's ideas.

Thirty teachers and administrators, including our Assistant Superintendent of Education and a board member, attended the National Middle School Conference in Louisville in the fall of 1991. Teachers from Blue Valley presented sessions on interdisciplinary teaming, advisement activities, and a variety of other related subjects at that conference. Back home in Blue Valley we continued reading the literature on integration, including the October 1991 issue of *Educational Leadership* on integrating the curriculum and the November 1991 and January 1992 issues of the *Middle School Journal* which focused on the curriculum question. Interest in integrated curriculum was growing, although there was certainly anxiety, and many questions remained unanswered.

Because it is critical that principals play a leadership role in innovation, whether organizational or curricular, we decided one more staff development opportunity was needed for our group before we could feel comfortable assisting teachers in implementing interdisciplinary and integrated units. In April of 1992 we attended an ASCD three day workshop in St. Louis that featured James Beane as the major consultant. We viewed videos that Beane and several teachers had developed to actually show students involved in the integrated curriculum process. More importantly, we talked directly with Beane about the integrated curriculum model and shared our feelings and fears about such a dramatic shift in curriculum and instruction. Each principal returned to his or her respective building with a wealth of resources and a new commitment to supporting teachers in this very important effort.

Curriculum integration will happen one school at a time, one team at a time. While the decision to change the organizational structure of middle schools from departmentalization to interdisciplinary teaming can, and often is, made from the district level, the integration of curriculum occurs through the willingness of individual teams to explore a different way of organizing their instruction, time, and expectations. It involves a willingness to trust students and listen to their thoughts and feelings about those issues and concerns that are most important to them. Joel Barker, the futurist, expressed the view that people resist paradigm change when it shows up too soon but that new paradigms are refound in times of crisis. We are certainly facing crises in our schools today. Perhaps that is why the core curriculum work of the 40s and 50s was not embraced as wholly as it deserved to be, but is now reappearing under the guise of integrated curriculum. As we educate our young adolescents to face the challenges of the future and join the work force of the twenty-first century, we must find new boundaries and let go of old paradigms. Middle schools, not surprisingly, are leading the way in real educational reform.

> **Curriculum integration will happen one school at a time, one team at a time.**

ONE TEAM'S STORY

We came together as a 6th grade team in the fall of 1990 with the opening of a the new Overland Trail Middle School of 700 students located in an affluent suburb of Kansas City. Organized into a five-person team, specialists in the areas of math, science, social studies, language arts, and reading, the five of us had not worked together previously. With a variety of backgrounds and experiences, we began to plan for the upcoming year, and each of us developed our own instructional methods based on the district curriculum for our specific content areas. However, we did incorporate common team goals and expectations for our students as well as ourselves. By accomplishing this, district expectations were met for team functioning and planning. These procedures continued throughout the fall semester.

As the fall progressed, a team personality developed and personal friendships were built among the five of us. Mutual trust was established, enabling us to take risks in curriculum and scheduling. During the first fall, we also examined our students' personalities and learning styles.

When the exploratory team in our building approached core teams for support with an upcoming February musical, "Teddy and Alice," we jumped at the chance to provide support by developing our first thematic unit on teddy bears. Our primary goal was to unify the school with a common theme of study.

The students experienced correlation among classes and, most importantly, that learning was fun! All five teachers developed their own activities that not only stayed within curriculum boundaries/objectives, but also allowed for spontaneity. For example, in reading students made 3-D bears by following oral directions. In math students worked with "teddy graham crackers" to develop concepts related to fractions.

Our common team planning period not only provided the time to plan the unit, but also to evaluate and critique it. Even though we believed that this experience was successful, we were assured of it when our students kept asking when the next thematic unit would take place. That validation was all the encouragement we needed, so we continued with more multidisciplinary or thematic units throughout the spring.

Before the year ended, we set a team goal to develop at least one thematic unit per month for the following school year. The administrators in our building had wholeheartedly supported our thematic units during the spring, and encouraged us to pursue our goals. Our efforts were directed towards choosing themes we felt were appropriate and of interest to students. As we met and worked together during the summer months, we found that developing these themes and activities was challenging, yet enjoyable, because of the creative freedom allowed. Content area objectives were also being met, which validated the time it took to plan and implement each unit.

While this collaboration review validated what we were doing among ourselves and the district, we also realized the need to inform our parents about the types of units we were doing and the reasons for doing them. We decided to include in our monthly parent newsletter information pertaining to theme activities and the objectives that would be met.

Our second year together began with much enthusiasm, and we found our new team of students was just as excited about learning from thematic units. Each unit focused on a team purpose as well as satisfying various district objectives. For example, we began the school year with a theme centered around *shoes*. Team-building activities, as well as academic activities, were designed including: welcome postcards sent to each student, color coded footprints that led the way to each team classroom, and students' footprints traced onto a team banner entitled, "Steppin' Into 6th Grade."

Upon asking ourselves what we learned from these early thematic units, a variety of responses arose.

I can meet my same objectives away from a textbook with hands-on activities.

Students eagerly partake in their learning, tearing down the 'you can't teach me' wall.

Teachers go the extra mile, we use our team planning time, individual planning time, and then some, but the reward of children actively learning is well worth the extra time we spend.

By the end of the first semester, with a number of short-term thematic units successfully completed, we were ready to evolve our thematic "Space Unit" into a fully integrated unit. Because we are fortunate enough to have established in our district solid blocks of team planning time, we were able to flex our schedule to accommodate an eighty-minute instructional time following the lunch break for this integrated unit. Before the lunch break students followed their normal schedule of classes which were shortened to thirty minutes each. Teachers used this time to enhance "space" activities within their own classrooms.

We developed this integrated space curriculum as a result of two of us receiving instruction in space science through the University of Kansas. The knowledge gained was brought back to the team and disseminated during planning time. It was imperative that all five of us felt secure in teaching this space unit as it incorporated information, concepts, and activities from all disciplines. It is outlined on the following pages and is followed by a description of a government and election unit.

Because we experienced considerable success implementing the space unit, we eagerly anticipated multiple integrated units for the upcoming school year. We have already begun this process by surveying our incoming sixth-graders as to their areas of interest and concerns, and we are ready to incorporate integrated units which address their questions and concerns. Our hope was that the curriculum would focus on learning opportunities for students based on current student-centered issues, as well as societal issues they will face.

This school year was a whole new ball game. Although we continued our thematic units on *Shoes, Hamburgers, Pizza,* and our teacher-designed *Mission Possible* integrated unit, we began a process wherein students give input to the year's curriculum.

An Integrated Curriculum Resource Unit

1. Title/theme: Mission Possible

2. Short description: This unit introduced students to the possibility of space travel by providing a unit of study which encompassed hands-on activities, promoted team learning problem solving, while stimulating curiosity and imagination.

3. Describe the "problem focus": Students worked cooperatively in groups known as flight crews to complete tasks which required problem solving and inquiry related to space travel and existence on the space shuttle.

4. Student generated questions and influences: An informal survey was conducted in reading class which indicated student desire to learn about the possibilities of life on other planets, space travel, and UFO's. Some questions that arose were, "Is there life in outer space?" "Can we live in space?"

5. Goals, major objectives: The overall goal was to expand students' perspectives of themselves, their communities, and ultimately their world. Major objectives included developing the students' ability to function as part of a group, to formulate and test hypotheses related to space travel, and to gain a working knowledge of shuttle procedures. By using measurement skills the children taped an outline of the shuttle mid-deck floor plan to the classroom floor. This increased the students' awareness of actual size of shuttle living space—smaller than many of their bedrooms. These skills reinforced in students our overall district goals related to problem solving, complex thinking, and communication.

6. Relationship of this unit to existing curriculum:
        Math—measurement, computation, geometry
        Reading—analysis, sequencing, reading for pleasure
        Language Arts—factual and creative writing, vocabulary study
        Science—gather and interpret data, hypothesize, observations
        Social Studies—community living in space, map skills, cultural constraints.

7. Activities:
        (a) initial—shuttle awareness pretest to assess prior knowledge.
        (b) ongoing—design flight crew logos and tee shirts, make styrofoam and paper shuttle models, simulation of space shuttle orbit utilizing slides an scripts, replicate shuttle mid-deck with masking tape on floor, develop personal preference kits that consist of items each student would take into space, learn how certain toys react in near zero gravity and design a toy to test in space.
        (c) culminating—test aerodynamics of styrofoam and paper shuttle model. "Space Night" when parents accompanied students to school to view completed projects.
        (d) evaluative—Bloom's test for evaluation taken in cooperative groups of flight crews: rotated to all five classrooms where they had the opportunity to choose specific questions and activities to complete; teachers generated these test items from the six levels of Bloom's taxonomy; a student evaluation was also conducted.

8. Resources and materials:
    Beane, James (1990). *A Middle School Curriculum: From Rhetoric to Reality.* Columbus, OH:
        National Middle School Association. (Second edition, 1993).
    Forte, Imogene and Schurr, Sandra (1992). *Cooperative Learning Guide and Planning Pak for*
        Middle Grades. Tampa, FL: National Resource Center for Middle Grades/High School
        Education.

Middle School Journal. November 1991 and January 1992. Columbus, OH: National Middle
   School Association.

"Red Planet Mars". Planetarium Program, University of California, Berkley.

"Remarkable Flying Machine," , Houston, TX: National Aeronautics and Space Administration.

Segal, Naomi. "Should We Go to Mars?" *Junior Scholastic*. September 20, 1991.

Teacher in Space Project. Houston, TX: National Aeronautics and Space Administration.

"Touching the Future". Challenger Center Teacher Workshop.

"Toys That Teach" (1986). Young Astronaut Program.

Contact for training:

> Challenger Center for Space Science Education,
> Suite 190, 1101 King Street,
> Alexandria, VA 22314.
> 1-800-969-5747

Contact for free and low-cost materials:

> NASA Spacelink, Marshall Space Flight Center
> Huntsville, Alabama 35807.
> voice: (205) 544-2121; modem: (205) 895-0028
>
> NASA Lewis Research Center
> Mail Stop 7-14, 2100 Bookpark Road,
> ATTN: Dr. R. Lynn Bondurant, Jr.
> Huntsville, Alabama 35807

9. *Responsibilities of team and individuals:*

teacher responsibilities:
—developing schedule, purchasing student materials,
—photocopying necessary student materials and student handbooks daily
—previewing and evaluating of activities, lab preparation for experiments,
—organization of student flight crews, setting up displays for Space Night.

student responsibilities:
—participate in activities by flight crews, bring in consumable materials, as well as art supplies needed for projects, turning in completed activities according to specified timeline, setting up displays for Space Night.

10. *Comments on the unit:*

Because this was our first attempt at full integration, parent involvement was limited to attending Space Night and providing refreshments for this event. We look toward this as an area of expansion next year. Community resources included information and support from Dr. Walter Smith, Professor of Science, Department of Education, University of Kansas, and Wendell Mohling, President of the National Science Teachers' Association.

From the student evaluative surveys collected at the conclusion of the unit, we found student knowledge increased most significantly from hands-on activities and participation in simulations. Students also expressed increased confidence in their ability to function and work within a group setting.

An Integration Government and Election Unit

Students on the 6 Maroon Team went through a process at the beginning of the year in which they were asked to write down and share questions they had about themselves and the world around them to create a list of common themes they would like to study throughout the year. A theme of government, elections, and presidents was requested by the students. Because of its timeliness teachers and students together decided that this theme would follow our first integrated unit, which focused on natural disasters.

Student Empowerment

Students worked in small groups to develop common questions they had related to government, elections, and presidents. Then they suggested lists of activities that could be done by students to help them find answers to their questions. Students were also asked to list their activities by subject disciplines (i.e., math, social studies, science, reading, language arts, and exploratory classes).

During the integrated unit, students choose what classroom they would like to work in, as well as the amount of time spent on each assignment. The following paragraphs provide information on the activities to be completed by each student and/or student groups.

Curriculum

Students developed activities that would help them find answers to their questions about the government.

Math

After reviewing a U.S. map displaying the number of electoral votes each state possesses, students will develop fractions and the corresponding percentages of each state in relation to the entire country and the total number of electoral votes. Examples and instruction will be done in class. Students will also be required to construct one type of graph (i.e., line, bar, or circle) that depicts data/information related to government, elections, and presidents. Various criteria for each type of graph will be discussed in class. Finally, students will have the opportunity to complete an election night activity sheet where they will chart the electoral votes obtained by each candidate as the election returns are reported.

Science

To prepare for a "Presidents Parade," students will research one president's life. A short paper will be written and presented orally, including different facts about the president's life, emphasizing his health, and will pinpoint a specific scientific discovery or invention during that president's term of office. When giving the oral presentations, students will be asked to dress in the appropriate attire of the era and/or develop props appropriate to their president's life.

Language Arts

Students will participate in three activities. After discussing the constitution, students will work with a partner to develop their own constitution centered around school, team, and individual rights and responsibilities. Second, students will choose one of the following topics to research: 1) one paragraph on who the student would vote for and why, 2) one paragraph describing what the student would do if elected president, and 3) a paragraph explaining why meeting the president would be a valuable experience. Finally, all students will take a spelling test of twenty presidents' first and last names.

Social Studies

All students will receive an election packet that contains information on political parties, key issues, candidates, and the electoral process. After studying the information, students will demonstrate their understanding of material by creating one of the following: 1) word search with definition of words, 2) crossword puzzle, or 3) election '92 board game. After investigating different forms of government, students will use an atlas and world almanac to identify a minimum of 50 countries on a world map and indicate their form of government. Students will also have a choice for extra credit by either creating a timeline of the presidents, or completing an activity sheet on presidents' nicknames and campaign slogans.

Reading

Students will read the biographies of the three presidential candidates. A comparison/contrast chart will then be constructed noting personal data and opinions about current political issues. Students will then rank the candidates in personal preference order of 1, 2, 3, and support their decisions with a written statement. Secondly, each student will be required to complete a political/campaign poster using one of eight previously learned persuasion techniques. Finally, students will read about the history and design of the White House, then complete a construction timeline for the structure. Extra credit points will be offered to each student who participates in a group construction of a scale model of the White House.

Evaluation

Evaluation measures for the unit consist of: 1) student booklets which will contain individual projects for each class listed above; 2) Oral presentations focusing on the president each student researched; and 3) Self-evaluations completed by students regarding the unit as a whole.

After finishing integrated units on Natural Disasters, Government-Elections, Rain Forest, World Peace, and Health, students once again gave their input through informal evaluation. Following are some of their thoughts.

We had choice about what we wanted to learn.

We got to try new/different approaches to learning.

Other people cared enough about what we were doing that they came to visit. The media were also involved several times. Barbara Bush came to visit.

We used teamwork to accomplish goals.

We are proud of our work and the projects we produced.

With those sincere student comments, how could we choose not to continue toward achieving a fully integrated curriculum in the years ahead? →

7

First Steps Toward Curriculum Integration: Using Student Questions

Sharon Craig, Roger DeLong, Jerry Nichols, Kevin Brown, Ronald Grover, Sheila Nemer, Susan Beaulier, Mary Bushey, David Morrow, Gene Brown. and Terry Despres

Located in rural Maine, Ashland Middle School is new to middle level philosophy. This school spent two years studying issues of adolescent development and curriculum issues before attempting curriculum reform. Grounded in common beliefs, the school has worked to solidify adult relationships in teams as the basis for curriculum integration. The struggle has produced significant results in student learning and teacher growth.

The Ashland Middle School (ME), in its fifth year of development, serves eighty students in grades seven and eight. The school is part of the Ashland School District serving the Ashland, Portage, Garfield Plantation, Masardis, and Oxbow Plantation communities where the economic base is largely lumber and forest products. The middle school is located in the same building as Ashland Community High School and shares common facilities and some programs.

Staff development

The principal, Terry Despres, has promoted middle level education for four years. Based on a staff needs assessment, he organized a five day training program in middle level education. Curriculum reform was determined to be the priority area in the movement to becoming a middle level school. Resistance to middle level education concepts was minimized following participation of the Middle School Planning Team in this five day in-service program during fall, 1990. It was the foundation for changing attitudes toward curriculum change and succeeded in developing a sense of cohesiveness and purpose among its members. It also began to address issues of staff isolation resulting from subject isolation. One staff member was quoted as saying, "It is exciting to team. We see purpose and cohesiveness in our daily teachings."

Because of size and cost limitations faced by a small school and realizing the potential professional benefits of inter-school collaboration, Mr. Despres organized a network of six small rural schools in Aroostook County for the purpose of participating in middle level staff development activities.

A member administrator reflected, "Teacher training should follow this format. Schools of common concern can lend positive staff development activities to each other. This cohort group has nurtured the spirit for learning." Staff development activities have included various topics of adolescent development, change, integrated curriculum, thematic learning, grouping, as well as teaching and learning strategies.

Curriculum change

The collaborative staff development project was the catalyst needed to move toward integrated, student-centered curriculum planning.

Ashland Middle School was ready for renewal and change. The collaborative staff development project was the catalyst needed to encourage the curriculum committee to move toward integrated, student-centered curriculum planning. It was innovative, not in the curriculum design itself, but in the way teachers designed the curriculum in time and context. Not a one-shot event, but an ongoing practice, it was integrated, because research indicates that students learn best in this manner. It was student-centered so the curriculum had meaning and relevance to the student. The success of its development could provide a model for future middle school curricula. A network science teacher noted, "It only makes sense to integrate. Students see linkage and I feel professional and in control. Teaming allows my philosophy to be understood by the team and I understand theirs."

Research and the collective reflections of teachers have made it evident that traditional classroom instructional strategies must be modified. Lower achieving students taught in homogeneous classes often develop low self-concepts which manifest themselves in minimal effort and learning. Incorporating this research and local observation, the planning team developed a unit which would provide an opportunity for students of all perceived levels to share in a common endeavor.

A student survey was administered to determine students' interests in social, personal, and health issues, as well as types of activities they would like to complete in studying these issues. The planning team used this information to determine the theme and related projects for the week.

The initial survey of middle school students' interests and concerns was distributed in class. Initially teachers were highly resistant in allowing students to suggest classroom curriculum. However, they were very responsive to the needs that arose through the survey. Perhaps the initial resistance resulted from concerns about drastic changes they feared would be imposed upon them by school administrators? If some resistance and tension were not present, it is unlikely that change would have occurred. The results of the student interest survey were then used to determine the theme of the curriculum project. Student concerns about the future, their health, and the environment were used to determine the final "Energy" theme of the project.

A wide variety of activities were planned for the week to implement the goals and objectives collaboratively agreed upon by the team during common planning time. They included the following goals and objectives with some indication of means of achieving them:

1. To increase students' knowledge of energy sources using charts, graphs, discussions, data research, and debates.
2. To locate geographically, with student-generated maps, energy sources and the areas in which they are most useful.
3. To chart and graph statistical information garnered from information generated throughout the week.
4. To discuss the pros and cons of various sources of energy through the use of collages, researched essays, vocabulary development, and debate.
5. To demonstrate ways in which various energy sources can be transformed into electrical energy by constructing models of power plants.
6. To increase their cooperative learning, decision-making, problem solving, and listening skills by participating in team and/or group activities.

During the planning phase for the activities, connections between the "Energy" unit and the school's core curriculum were identified. Initial activities included promoting student awareness through posters and student surveys. Teachers prepared for the unit by meeting daily with students in heterogeneous groups, gathering materials, and discussing timelines.

The primary difference between this curriculum and the traditional curriculum was that students were the researchers and ultimately the teachers. They took on the responsibility of posing their own questions and answering them through a group problem-solving approach. The primary responsibility for the classroom teacher was to act as a facilitator for the student research-based curriculum. As facilitator, the teacher often took on the role of listener, advisor, occasional referee, and overseer of projects.

The success of an integrated thematic unit is not dependent upon the efforts of a small number of students. Success lies in the total involvement of all components within this unit; planning team, individual instructors, outside professionals, and students.

Energy week

Students were grouped heterogeneously into six groups of thirteen members. At least one member of each group was recognized by the planning team as having leadership potential, although each team member was expected to contribute to the group effort, and the group as a whole decided what each member would contribute. Group collaboration and achievement was stressed.

Each group was assigned one of the following forms of energy: solar, nuclear, hydro, fossil fuel, geothermal, and biomass. The groups of thirteen broke into separate groups of three or four to research different topics pertaining to their energy form. Groups worked on topics such as economic feasibility, geographic location, use of local resources, pollution, and special problems caused by each energy source. The outcome was a review of commonly used energy sources to determine which were most environmentally friendly and economically practical for any given area.

Each teacher on the team was assigned one of the energy groups. It was the obligation of that individual to ensure that a final presentation by that group would be completed for the energy fair to be held on the last day of the unit. Instructors were responsible for helping students plan individual activities to be displayed and/or presented at the energy fair. Every instructor helped secure extra materials required to complete classroom projects. This work was done in classrooms, the media center and the community. Students wrote essays, developed debate teams, made models of energy plants, and prepared charts and graphs, among other activities.

In science class, students constructed models of energy producing plants. This activity required students to demonstrate a variety of skills varying from computation to electrical construction. Construction of graphs, maps, and charts in the social studies area increased their knowledge of Maine's and the nation's energy supplies. Mathematical skills were heightened by compiling statistics and developing graphs and charts. This led to an increased knowledge of geometry, percentages, and data analysis. Through theme writing in reading and English classes, students increased their research, writing, debating, and vocabulary development skills. Students were encouraged to apply the basic knowledge of each learning area in the development of their group projects.

The energy week concluded with an energy fair. A half day project to clean up the local community began the fair. This activity was designed to give students a sense of environmental responsibility and an appreciation for their community. During the second half of the energy fair, all six energy groups presented their projects to the other middle school students. Positive recognition was given to students by televising part of the energy fair on the local news channel and awarding certificates of appreciation to each student.

Theme week involved nearly 100% student participation in all activities. After witnessing the success of the students and studying survey results, the middle school teachers pronounced the project beneficial for all involved. Perhaps the team's greatest learning was in recognizing the value of using integrated units and making the commitment to continue with this approach to curriculum development and delivery.

The media center was crucial to the success of this project. Media technicians acted as valuable resources of information for students and teachers alike. They worked with students, gathering research materials.

Assessment of the unit

Student reaction—A student survey was distributed immediately following the presentations, and 76 surveys were collected. Sixty-four percent of the students indicated that they learned more than they did through their usual curriculum format and 24% stated that they learned as much as the regular curriculum. Twelve percent of the students said they learned less than in the usual curriculum format. When asked how often they would like to do this type of activity, 43% stated all the time, 34% stated at least twice a year, 16% stated once a year, and 7% stated that they would not like to do this activity at all.

When asked how much practical knowledge was gained in this project, 49% said that they gained a lot, 46% stated that they gained some practical knowledge, and 5% said they gained no practical knowledge.

Some teachers were initially skeptical about student participation. A survey comment by a middle school teacher was germane: "I was worried that the activities we would use would involve only a few students. I learned that students involve other students when they team. They know the value of teaming. Boy was I wrong..." Concerns by the teachers that only a few students would do all the work were not substantiated by the survey results. Seventy-four percent of the students indicated that they did "a lot" of work and 24% of the students stated that they did "some work." Only 2% of the students stated that they did not work at all. When asked who did the most work, 61% of the students stated that everyone did a lot, 18% stated that a small group did the most, 12% stated that they did the most, and 9% stated that someone else did the most work. Eighty-seven percent of the students agreed, however, that the best results are obtained when the entire group is involved.

Eighty-seven percent of the students agreed that the best results are obtained when the entire group is involved.

Another positive aspect of the project noted by school personnel was the significant reduction in absenteeism during that week. During the week of the project, there were only three absences, and on the day of the energy fair, there were two absences. This indicated a decrease in absenteeism from 20% to 4% per week during this unit.

Teacher reaction—The Middle School Teacher Survey, administered confidentially, revealed several changes in attitude toward heterogeneous grouping. There was strong support toward heterogeneous grouping at the beginning of the year with three of five teachers strongly favoring it and two mildly favoring it. The two teachers who mildly favored heterogeneous grouping became strongly supportive as a result of this endeavor.

Comments by the teachers suggested that they could see the benefits as well as the difficulties of this practice. The project allowed teachers to experience heterogeneous grouping and have input into the decision-making process. Teachers and administrators decided that the middle school will be totally heterogeneously grouped during the next school year.

The survey asked the teachers about the importance of planning integrated curriculum as a team. Four of the six teachers believed it was very important, one teacher thought it was critically important, and one felt it was not very important. All the teachers responded that students learned as much or more than in the regular program. Four of six teachers stated that the students learned more than in the regular program. All teachers were willing to implement an integrated curriculum approach again, with a majority willing to do so two or three times a year. The teachers were much more favorable toward a partially integrated curriculum. Four of the teachers were willing to work together on a monthly basis, and two were willing to work together on a weekly basis.

The survey reflected great strides in teachers' outlook in their ability to communicate with one another and cooperate in planning curriculum. At the beginning of the year, they felt that their interactions were fair or not very good. By the end of the year, one teacher stated that it was fair and five teachers stated that it was very good.

When asked their opinions about what influences the curriculum the most, they all placed student needs as the biggest influence. Other influences were student opinion, administrative desires, teacher philosophy, educational techniques, staffing, and building space. Ashland Middle School used block scheduling for the 1993-94 school year, which allowed for more curriculum integration opportunities.

Reflections

The changes resulting from our work have been gradual, yet significant. Although at times difficult to measure, many new instructional practices and strategies emerged as we have confronted traditionally held beliefs about school and curriculum.

1. Middle school curricula continues to be difficult to define and this is a great barrier to change. Many organizational changes as well as modifications in delivery of the curriculum have resulted from our attempts at defining what the curriculum should be. The comfortable past, as well as mandates from various local and state sources, also contribute to the tension that exists with change.

2. A major outcome of our pilot project with integrated curriculum has been movement away from homogeneous grouping and the will to investigate what young adolescent students really need for their healthy development. The debate about grouping has moved to a higher level with students' needs having priority over organizational practices.

3. Teaming provides for better continuity of curriculum delivery. Interdisciplinary teaming only assures good planning. Ashland Middle School must now move to true integrated units. There remains, however, a resistance to incorporate this into daily practice. Content versus process is a major debate in this area.

4. Maine's Educational Assessment (MEA) testing program has provided evidence of school improvement. Based upon this testing, Ashland Middle School has been given "Star" school status, an award provided to schools who show three year average test score improvements. Portfolios, demonstrations, and projects used to measure skills and knowledge learned by students have been encouraged, although more work needs to be done in this area to demonstrate continuing growth.

5. The emergence of the principal as an educational leader rather than a building manager, has had a significant impact. Teams must be provided the motivation and resources to change. Common planning time, staff development activities and philosophical support are examples of administrative backing. The principal must be ready and willing to make such major changes. Effective practice at the highest levels must be the expectation and it must be supported and rewarded by school administrators.

6. Parents are the greatest supporters of curriculum change. Informing and encouraging parents to be involved generates dividends of support. The informed parent becomes a strong advocate for continuing change, while parent voices with the Board of Education provide the foundation for the transition process. We have learned that to inform parents is more than telling the parents. Parent nights and newsletters have their value, but actually involving parents with planning,

The informed parent becomes a strong advocate for continuing change.

learning through interdisciplinary activities, and participating on teams results in strong advocacy for middle level programs.

7. The changes for Ashland Middle School have placed new stress as well as many opportunities on our secondary program. Students who have learned in this model expect similar learning once they reach the high school. This points out the need to train secondary staff alongside the middle school staff. High school teachers must develop their own practice and resist the middle school label for their change process. The sensitive administrator recognizes this and uses new terminology for similar practices at the secondary level. Teaming is not the same as it is in the middle school. The two concepts have inherent similarities but somewhat diverse practices.

8. An additional benefit of our experience is the clear identity for the middle level program. Middle school teachers no longer view their school as simply a transitional one, as the training ground for the high school. They respect their new identity and see a clear mission of providing for the developmental needs of the learner.

The middle level experience affects attitudes about how we learn. Terry Despres concludes... "I have seen many changes in my twenty-five plus years as an educator, but none have impacted the learning atmosphere as has this program. We have only begun the change process. My parents, staff, and most of all my students, believe in what they are doing. So do I." ➔

8 | TWENTY YEARS LATER: MULTIDISCIPLINARY TO INTEGRATED UNITS.

Charlene Carper

McKelvie Middle School, Bedford, New Hampshire, has provided its students with interdisciplinary/integrated approaches to curriculum for twenty years. Their success with the Cardigan Unit has led them to other integrated units which supplemented the curriculum; now, curriculum integration is becoming "the" curriculum. In addition, teachers are focusing on assessment strategies consistent with integrated curriculum.

Ingredients for success

- A staff committed to the child and middle level philosophy.
- Two pods that are advanced in team development
- A staff that is open to using what research tells us about teaching and learning practices.

Since the mid-seventies, the eighth grade staff at the McKelvie Middle School has mixed together the aforementioned ingredients and provided their students an educational experience that includes two integrated, interdisciplinary units/themes. Each of these units has continued to evolve as the third ingredient has changed. At the present time each unit comprises approximately one quarter of students' eighth grade year. During these units, flexible grouping (large and small), cooperative learning, advisor/advisee, hands-on experience, real life connections and experiences, along with alternative assessment, all come into play. Additionally, themes from each of these units are incorporated into activities and lessons during the two remaining quarters of the school year.

The school where it happens

The McKelvie Middle School is located in an upper middle class community of approximately 12,000 people. The 890 pupil school, housing grades 5-8, is divided into pods at each of the grade levels. This enables a relatively large school to offer a smaller environment for the students. Pods range in size from two to five professionals. Throughout the school, students are heterogeneously grouped with the exception of pre-algebra in the 7th grade and algebra in the 8th grade. This heterogeneous population includes special needs students and the school's gifted and talented program staffed by one professional who services all students in the 5th and 6th grades as well as identified students in the 7th grade. This service is provided both in a teaming situation with regular education teachers as well as whole class instruction and pull-out program provided by the gifted and talented teacher.

All subjects taught at the McKelvie Middle School have written curriculums. In developing integrated units, these curricula serve as a resource regarding skills and content progression for grades K-8. While the present configuration of the school and the total school population was different at the time of the inception of the two integrated units now taught, the basic environment that allowed these units to develop, continues to aid, assist, and support them.

How were these units developed, how and why has the evolution continued, and what has been the community's reaction? These topics are all part of the Cardigan and Consumer Units story.

The basics

When these units were initially developed, there were no models to use. The staff recognized a need, brainstormed an idea, and proceeded. Yearly, the themes were assessed by the staff using both student and teacher input. What worked, what did not, how could it have been done better? Over the years as more research has been done the staff has incorporated new strategies into their lessons and into the construction of the units so as to best meet the needs of all students. In the past few years, the research on learning styles, cooperative learning, and learning by doing has had a great impact on the ongoing development of these units. This curriculum is indeed a living, breathing one.

The assessment piece has been the slowest to develop. However, in the past two years, an alternative assessment has been used and has been well received. One staff member stated, "We have developed a unique report card that communicates progress made toward the educational goals of the unit rather than just a letter grade in a subject matter."

The Cardigan Unit

The Cardigan Unit began in the 1970s during a process of revising the science curriculum. The eighth grade science teachers wanted to provide "exciting, hands-on" experiences for their students. During their pod meeting time, the eighth grade teachers brainstormed some ideas which resulted in the idea of involving students, parents, and community leaders to develop an interdisciplinary unit of instruction.

From the "brainstorming" beginnings, the science coordinator set out to inform and include various constituencies. In addition, he made sure that the principal and the Assistant Superintendent for Curriculum and Instruction were an integral part of the process. This administrative support was critical. Summer curriculum development was used, allowing the program to become part of the district's program and consequently the district funding process.

As Bob Little, principal at the time, wrote, "Ray Landry , the Science Coordinator, did the following:

1. He recognized a need and then did some brainstorming.
2. He kept administrators at the local and front office level aware and involved.
3. He developed a strategy to get others involved (i.e., his peers, students, school board)
4. He used an existing vehicle, curriculum development, to accomplish his goal.
5. He built in an evaluation model and continued to keep people involved and informed."

Out of these initial discussions and meetings an interdisciplinary unit on the environment was developed, which has since evolved into a broader unit focused on stewardship.

In a continuing effort to keep parents and students informed about the unit, teachers wrote the Cardigan Manual; the goals and objectives of the Cardigan unit, as detailed in the manual, follow.

Interdisciplinary approach

The main objective of this unit is to provide through an interdisciplinary approach a first-hand study of environmental phenomena and problems to all eighth grade students at McKelvie Middle School. The unit will emphasize those aspects of each discipline which contribute to the basic understanding of, and concern for, the interaction of man with his total environment.

Direct experience

Through opportunities for students to be in the out-of-doors, an understanding of various environmental components and their interrelationships will be achieved. Man's ability to alter environments and the long-term effects of these alterations will be stressed.

Through these experiences in the out-of-doors, students will begin to understand the complexity of environmental problems, the necessity to solve these problems from a broad base of knowledge, and a recognition of the importance of the environment to man's affective nature. This experience will provide students with the opportunity to interact directly with natural phenomena, fellow students, and adults in developing a sense of responsibility to all living things and the physical environment.

Educational goals

1. Successfully complete pre-planned tasks and projects.
2. Develop cooperative techniques in completing group projects.
3. Establish criteria to more objectively evaluate man's place within the environment.
4. Recognize the interdependence of all living things and give specific examples of such relationships.
5. Perceive the dynamic nature of all biological communities and the physical world.
6. Recognize and understand that all living things are a product of their heredity and environment.
7. Precisely define ecological terms and concepts.
8. Increase understanding of man's place in the biophysical environment.
9. Identify potential career choices and assess one's skills, interests, and abilities in relation to these areas.
10. Increase understanding of the need to adapt to varied situations.
11. Recognize learning as a totality instead of a fragmented body of skills.
12. Increase sensitivity to and interest in many environmental factors and dynamics.
13. Develop communication and interpersonal skills both with peer groups and adults.
14. Increase self-reliance and leadership skills.

As indicated earlier, each student receives a Cardigan Manual, a working textbook authored by the 8th grade staff. The staff makes revisions every summer, so it is always up-to-date. By developing all the materials used in the unit, the staff has exactly what they want and need for students. To date, they have not found any commercial materials that better meet the needs of students. Developing their own materials has also resulted in ownership by all staff members.

In its evolution, the unit has been four weeks, six weeks, and nine weeks duration. This change in time has been a result of new components being added, expanded pre-Cardigan activities, and incorporating new teaching and learning strategies. Each year is different.

Additional ingredients—teachers change too

Each teacher's role in this eighth grade curriculum continues to change. The role has changed from being predominantly a teacher of content to being a teacher of all students in all content areas, and this too is an ever evolving process. The homeroom teacher is the camp group leader and the students are his/her camp group. This structure has led to a strong advisor/advisee style program. As the camp group leader, teachers have become responsible for all phases of their students' education.

The role has changed from being a teacher predominantly of content to being a teacher of all students in all content areas.

The teachers have also made a commitment to continue learning. One strategy used by the staff is to have the "experts" in the field being studied present information in a large group setting to both students and staff. The camp group leader (staff member) reinforces that learning, and students practice using it in the camp group setting. Using cooperative learning groups has assisted in facilitating success for all learners.

Components of assessment

After a visit to McKelvie School by Jim Beane and a conversation he had with the 8th grade staff, these professionals pointed out to the administration the incongruence of the traditional form of student reporting and the intent of an integrated curriculum. As a result of this exchange, the staff developed new reporting forms. The mid-term progress report now provides information on specific activities of the unit along with quiz and test scores. The affective components of the curriculum are also addressed. The report card gives one academic average along with other pertinent information. This move toward a more holistic approach has been well received. Parental understanding has come through a presentation made by the 8th grade staff at the annual Open House. This presentation included research that supports such a change.

With each staff member being responsible for the educational program of his/her homeroom, they all share in the responsibilities associated with the unit in their camp group. Staff meet daily, make large group presentations, facilitate learning of students, and assess achievement. In addition, staff members continually assess the unit on a daily and yearly basis. One staff member commented that "any unit must be put together by the staff members who will be implementing it." This can exist even with new staff coming into the grade because of the continuing assessment of the unit. The yearly and daily planning allows even the newest staff member to have input into the components of the unit and how these will be organized for the year.

Because these units are the curriculum for the eighth grade, there is district financial support for them through the regular budgetary process. This reinforces the fact that integrated curriculum is valued in the educational program.

The consumer unit

The second unit was developed more than fifteen years ago as a result of a discussion between a math teacher and a social studies teacher on the topic of consumerism. Its development has somewhat paralleled that of the Cardigan Unit with the various disciplines becoming a part of the unit as natural connections emerged. Using a real-life simulation format, the following are objectives of the Consumer Unit:

1. Identify and use all terms covered in the unit.
2. Be familiar with all occupations covered and discussed in class.
3. Know how to figure their net pay (weekly, monthly, and yearly) by deducting their Social Security and Federal Withholding Tax.
4. Set up and use a working budget.
5. Identify various careers through presentations from community members.
6. Utilize library materials and various classroom resources.
7. Understand percents and show how they relate to buying and selling.
8. Calculate percents and show how they relate to buying and selling.
9. Compare the different budget areas by making a circle graph.
10. Explore career choices through the use of interviewing techniques.
11. Understand how the consumer can indirectly effect his/her economic condition.
12. Be exposed to and be familiar with the following:
    a. social security form
    b. lease application
    c. all insurances
    d. taxes
    e. job application
    f. mortgage procedure
    g. car loan and car title
    h. car title
    i. guarantees/warranties
    j. W-2 form (short form)
    k. basic banking forms and procedures
13. Be able to identify the difference between the economic systems of capitalism, socialism, and communism.
14. Demonstrate an understanding of the American free enterprise system or capitalism.
15. Become familiar with the buying and selling techniques in the stock market.

The activities for this unit are outlined on the progress report. These include: salary conversion, budget worksheets, final budget, mortgage, lease agreement, job application, cover letter, resumé, writing a check, car payment worksheet, taxation worksheet, two balance sheets, electric meter reading, salary conversion, lease agreement, electric bill, and balancing.

Teaching strategies employed are similar to those used in the Cardigan Unit with the exception of camp groups. For this unit, each teacher has a certain number of cooperative learning groups which he/she facilitates in the learning process. They too become a form of Advisor/Advisee group. Community involvement is also an integral part of this unit. Community members are asked to assist in the career portion, the accounting portion, the real estate sales, and others. Once again, the assessment piece has changed. Because there are no actual classes in math, language arts, science, and social studies, the student reporting system is also holistic for this unit.

Recommendations

What recommendations do these eighth grade teachers have for other professionals moving toward integrated curriculum? Make sure you have or make the TIME necessary. Time is needed for the development of the unit, the implementation segment, and for the assessment piece.

Make sure you have or make the TIME necessary.

While the eighth grade staff currently has ten planning periods every six days, they did not have that amount of daily time during the first years of these units. They used after-school time and summer time to meet. With the exception of the initial summer curriculum development time on the Cardigan Unit, the staff has not been financially compensated for their after school or summer work. These professionals felt and continue to feel so strongly about the benefits to students from this type of unit that they continue to give of their time without additional financial compensation.

Including all the stakeholders in the development process and in the ongoing units is also recommended. This has assisted in assuring the success of each unit. The ongoing involvement of these stakeholders is particularly important as the units are revised. Flexible scheduling and the willingness of team members to compromise and to be consistent are other important components needed for success. One staff member stated, "Teamwork is the basic answer to obstacles. Through mutual assistance and time, problems are solved." Thus the fifth stage in team development is demonstrated.

Finally, there is the need for individuals to continue professional development and to share their understandings with the group. Every staff member does not need to attend a professional development activity to gain from it. Sharing as a part of teamwork benefits everyone. This professional development attitude provides not only for staff renewal but also the best learning environment for students. →

9

INTERDISCIPLINARY STUDY IN A TECHNOLOGY EDUCATION CLASS

John Kraljic

Garland Street Middle School in Bangor, Maine, has had the programmatic elements of middle schools for 12 years. In this honest report, John Kraljic, technology education teacher, details an experiment into integrated curriculum he and his partner tried with a particular class. It is a good example of two teachers who learned from their students, once they allowed (and expected) them to perform at high levels without undue amounts of teacher direction.

Located near the center of the state, Bangor is Maine's second largest city. The school district consists of 10 schools: one 9-12 high school, two 6-8 middle schools, two 4-5 schools, and five K-3 schools. The Garland Street Middle School serves approximately one-half of the city's middle level students. The majority of the students who attend the Garland Street School are from middle to upper middle class families. Compared to similar schools in Maine and across the country, Garland Street students consistently perform well on standardized tests.

Ever since the Garland Street School changed from a 7-9 junior high school to a 6-8 middle school, the staff has been organized into teams. Most of the teams are organized by grade level, with one multi-grade (7/8) team and a unified arts team. With the exception of grade six and the multi-grade 7/8 team, teachers generally teach only one content area and students move from 45 minute class to 45 minute class during a seven period day. During the 1991-92 school year, students were randomly grouped for homeroom and then regrouped for individual classes.

A conversation with our school's gifted and talented coordinator/teacher during the Spring of 1990, gave birth to an idea for a special gifted and talented class, "to explore the history, current state, and future direction of technological development through interdisciplinary study." By the start of school in September, the seventh grade "Interdisciplinary Class" had been developed, coordinated with the other middle school; as often happens, each school had a new gifted and talented coordinator/teacher. During that first year, Ken Bonstein and I team taught twenty-two gifted and talented students four or five days a week throughout the year. Since this class was new, it provided a great opportunity to try new ideas within the guidelines of technological development.

During the 1991-92 school year, I enrolled in a graduate program at the University of Maine. In the middle level curriculum course, I read Jim Beane's book, *A Middle School Curriculum: From Rhetoric to Reality* (1990a), which raised the question of, "What ought to be the middle level curriculum?" In another middle level course, I read Chris Stevenson's, *Teaching Ten to Fourteen Year Olds* (1992), which provides many ideas for delivering and implementing the middle school curriculum. These courses, along with support from Ken, the school administration, and the students led to the following unit.

Some of the most valuable information came not from the work the students did, but from their comments in reflective essays.

In looking back on the unit, some of the most valuable information came not from the actual work the students did, but from the comments they made in a reflective essay. I was surprised by the quality and insight of the comments. Prior to this experience, when I read a professional article with "student comments" my reaction was, "students don't really make those kinds of comments and show that much insight." I learned otherwise. In this article, a number of student comments (italicized in the text) are included to give a flavor for some of the insights they had during this unit. Student comments and recommendations are extremely valuable, especially those from students who analyzed and reflected not only on what they produced but on the process they used.

Getting started

One of the requirements for the methods/implementation course was to "try-out" some of the ideas we read about. In one chapter of Chris Stevenson's book he discusses many different types of curriculum. While I'm not sure as to whether I'd classify it as an *exploratory study,* or as an *orbital/expert study,* I decided to try IT out. As an introduction, I talked with our interdisciplinary learning (IDL) class about education and some of the recent criticism schools and teachers have received on all fronts. In an attempt to correct some of these problems, I asked if they would like a part in selecting what they studied. Of course they were excited about the prospect of being able to choose what they studied and all began to talk at me at once. Realizing that we had to ease into this endeavor, I asked them to think about some possible topics and to write in their journals what they felt about this idea. I also asked them to jot down one or two topics that they might want to investigate.

When first assigned, I was overjoyed at the prospect of being able to work with such a wide range of topics. I still feel this was a good idea.

One of the best assignments all year. It gave us a chance to explore and broaden our horizons and find out about topics we never would have known very much about.

I enjoyed the last Interdisciplinary project. It was great to finally be able to choose your subject matter and manner of presenting it. On the other hand I didn't like having no guidelines. I kind of had to begin with no basis of what to do. There is really no way to avoid that though. Had there been a guideline to presenting your topic, the freedom would have been gone.

I recommend that more teachers give assignments like this with no/less boundaries. We should be given a choice of topics like in this project more often. I feel that they are more effective and fun.

The next day we provided more information about this "opportunity," including some of the guidelines. The guidelines were, from the teachers' perspective, extremely reasonable. The students would have four weeks for this activity, they could use almost all of their IDL class time and submit a daily journal. When all was said and done, we expected a written report, oral presentation to the class, and a three dimensional "artifact." It was at this point that the class realized that it wasn't a dream and that they were not about to go on a four week vacation for one period a day. It is amazing how, what appeared to be "the best thing since sliced bread" one day, turned into "another boring assignment" the next day.

This project resembled all the other projects that we have been assigned. They have all been the same. This is the problem with this assignment. The class might have enjoyed the assignment a little more if the expectations were changed.

My partner and I were probably as disappointed as the kids. What did they expect? Following a brief teacher talk on accountability, and sharing and reporting of information, complete with connections to the "real world," students were still unhappy. In an attempt to change the "us versus them" tension, I put the ball back into their court.

"Okay, here you have an opportunity to learn about something that you have an interest in. How can you demonstrate that you have actually learned and accomplished something and share that information with the class?" Ignoring the one person whose only suggestion was, "make it a study hall," after many false starts and comments like, "you two can watch us and you'll know what we deserve," the oral report, written report, and artifact were, at least partially, back in good graces.

"What do you want to investigate or learn more about?"

How does one select a single topic for research? This is the question the students struggled with for a couple of days. From the first day of this assignment, we had a student-generated list of possible topics. When I placed the list on the board, about a third of the class saw, "something that they *really* wanted to do."

Many students had a hard time getting started with this assignment. This is not necessarily bad, because selecting a topic, refining it, and setting the work parameters are always difficult tasks.

I really wish we could do a project like this again. It is interesting, fun, and educational, and we're learning about something that WE want to learn about, something that we think is interesting.

I would recommend that you leave this assignment the way it is. I feel that it has the right balance of guidelines and freedom. I feel that the presentations went over well and that letting us choose the subject allowed us enough space to do our best.

Our last project was much more fun in my opinion because we didn't have the strict guidelines.

I feel that the assignment we just did had both good and bad points. I learned a lot and I had a lot of fun. However, I do not believe that this project was presented very well. There was not much support from the teachers, and mine, along with most people's topics, was too large. Overall I enjoyed this project a lot. I learned a lot, and with a little fine tuning I would like to do it again.

At the end of the first week, some students were still unsure about exactly what their final topic was. Was this bad? I think both *yes* and *no*. For some students who began to gather information about a topic and modify their focus based on what they found, I think this uncertainty was fine. What they found guided them towards their ultimate goal.

I enjoyed the last interdisciplinary project. It was great to finally be able to choose your subject matter and manner of presenting it. On the other hand I didn't like having no guidelines. I kind of had to begin with no basis of what to do. There is really no way to avoid that though. Had there been a guideline to presenting your topic, the freedom would have been gone.

When first assigned, I was overjoyed at the prospect of being able to work with such a wide range of topics. I still feel this was a good idea except for the fact that some people received an insufficient amount of specific guidance as to their selection of main topics.

This was an assignment that was good in some ways and not so good in others. As you said, we had enough rope to hang ourselves. Some of us did just that. And some of us died pitifully slowly. My favorite part of this assignment was that I know more about my topic than anyone in the class.

I liked this assignment, in fact, it was probably my favorite out of all the assignments we have had. It gave me a chance to work with people that I wanted to, not who I was assigned to. I also liked the fact that I got to choose my topic. I have always felt that I do better work on something when I'm interested in it. I wanted to make the wind tunnel for a good grade and because I wanted to see it work.

I covered a wide range of subjects, I believe this may have reduced the quality of the presentation. Probably the instructors wanted the reports to be very specific.

I think I did average work for this assignment. I spent too much time at the beginning thinking about what I wanted to do. My model could have been better and I should have not waited for the last week to construct it.

On the other hand, there were students who had difficulty handling the freedom—the openness of the assignment and the way of operating in the classroom. They were the ones who would find someone who was doing something interesting and watch, or worse, interrupt and distract that person. These were the people who I feared, when the due date arrived, would not be ready and would have gained the least from this activity.

Some of the topics under investigation included: tropical fish, the human brain, flight, aerodynamics, birds, modern art, interpretative dance, HyperCard, Hawaii (guess where this student was going), pollution, sign language, and more. As for grouping, we allowed students to work either by themselves or with one other person. My colleague and I were uncertain where to draw the line between freedom to explore and academic accountability. On the accountability issue, we did require daily journal entries describing their progress, problems, successes and failures.

It would have helped if you had sat down with each group and just briefly discussed their plans with them. It would have helped many people finish this project with lots of time left.

The class presentations began at the end of March. On that first day, the presentations got off to a "business as usual" start. The presentations were little more than average, with students performing as they have in the past. The *modern art* artifacts were well done, but the oral reports dragged on in an attempt to "cover the material." The presentation on sign language was the best ever for the student, but the HyperCard maze lost the entire audience, and left everyone asking, "what's the point?" The students were probably more critical of their presentations than the instructors.

It wasn't the best presentation I've ever given. I didn't utilize my time to the best of my ability. My grades were satisfactory except I think that I deserve a higher mark on my written piece.

My project was okay. My project suffered because I couldn't find information ANYWHERE. My artifact stunk because I just changed subjects. Having more information also would have helped. I should have prepared more too.

I could have worked much harder. I gathered a large amount of information but then I never really took the time to look closely at that information. In other terms I was lazy.

The next day showed great improvements. The telling comment was from the person scheduled to present last that day. Quite concerned, he asked, "Do you mean I need to follow the colonization of Mars, an impressive working wind tunnel, and FOOD?" Fortunately for Adam, earlier presentations were long and he did a fine job with his presentation on architecture. Other highlights were: flightless birds (life size drawings, taped presentations , and an outstanding comic book on flightless birds); Hawaiian coral (complete with student made underwater slides); acupuncture, Egyptian burial methods, and more.

For the most part, Ken and I were quite pleased with the results. We saw some students do their best work of the year. I'm not saying that everything was perfect, but at the time, we felt that we would definitely do it again.

I believe I did very well on the entire assignment, considering some of the difficulties described above. On my presentation itself I feel I did well. My visuals helped me a lot in that I could never have put my presentation into words in such a short time without them.

Following the final presentation, we had a discussion with the class about the assignment. At first, some felt that there had been too much work. Pointing out that the only requirements were an oral presentation, an artifact, and a written piece, quickly defused that line of criticism. Others complained about having to do an oral presentation. These students ALWAYS complain about having to get up in front of the class. What concerned me most was that they direct so much energy to complaining about the oral presentation that they don't practice, don't organize, don't relax, don't listen to advice, and consequently deliver mediocre presentations.

I disliked this project immensely; actually, I didn't mind watching them, I just hated doing it myself. I actually liked it more when we had more guidelines. It's easier to do something when we know exactly what is expected of us, and how it should be done.

I liked seeing what other students had chosen for their projects when presentation time rolled around. There was such a variety.

The oral presentation went well for me. It did not go perfectly but finally all the speeches and presentations I have given in the last couple of months have paid off.

Another concern was student burn-out with their topic. Many of the students invested a great deal of time and energy into this project. So much that they grew tired or even sick of their topic and work. Again everyone needed to remember that they established their own guidelines. Did they bite off too much, or just do a good job?

I found that my topic was too broad. I narrowed the information down, but still there was a lot of information. Then I had to narrow it down again.

I would change two things: eliminate how long you wanted us to talk and give us more guidance. It was hard to know how much to do and exactly what to do.

I kind of hung myself. I did this to myself by doing a lot of research but when it came time to put it into a product, I had no idea of what to do. What I eventually did, didn't show everything that I knew about my topic. I think with more guidance my project would have been much better.

The high interest level was a definite motivating factor and the ability to set ones' own guidelines fostered not only a feeling of control, but also responsibility.

I was surprised by the assignment. This isn't the type of class that gives "limitless boundaries." The hardest part was the choosing of a topic.

The assignment was the most enjoyable project so far this year. We had the chance to learn about something of our own choice; something we actually wanted to know more about!

It is much more fun and interesting to learn about something you like. All in all I think that this was a very good project to do. I like it because it was fun.

Overall I think I did very well on my project, but I could have done better. You know how many times I changed my mind on what I should do, but it wasn't until after visiting the coral reef that I decided to do coral. Before visiting the reef I knew something about coral, but not much.

One of the most interesting questions I raised was, "Given the lack of concrete restrictions (written report to be 7 typed pages, oral report to be exactly 5 minutes long, etc.) did any of you do any less work?" All responses confirmed that students had done more work because they were interested in the topic.

I thought this assignment was fun. It gave us an opportunity to research what we like. The class had a chance to do what they wanted, which made it easier and made the task more fun. Since this project had few limits, we were all more interested in our topics, and therefore did a better job. It was also more enjoyable to watch our classmates' presentations because of their enthusiasm toward the assignment. This project was better than some in the past, due to its unique guidelines.

I came out with more than I expected. I realize that I learned a lot from this.

I thought the boundaries on this project were fair and it gave us the freedom to explore our subject creatively.

It was not easy to make the wind tunnel, especially all of those stupid straws, and the magazine also took a good amount or time to make, but it was worth it. I got a good grade, learned a lot, and had a pretty good time doing it.

> **Maybe someday they'll get the message that school is intended to help them do their best possible work, not torment them.**

This was an interesting class group. Some students just love to talk, some just to argue. Others will start talking and in mid-stream completely change their original position. Realizing that it would be impossible to obtain meaningful data from an oral discussion, we asked them to write an essay evaluating the assignment, their performance, and recommendations that would have made the assignment work better for them. When first assigned, the essay due date was Monday. A few students mentioned that they didn't feel they had enough time due to work for other classes. When I offered to accept the essays on Tuesday, the same skeptics couldn't believe that there would be no late penalty and were sure we would grade harder. My final blow to their skepticism came when someone jokingly mentioned Wednesday and I agreed that Wednesday would be the due date for all of the essays. Maybe someday they'll get the message that school is intended to help them do their best possible work, not torment them. Unfortunately, before students can realize this, schools need to become more aware of and change many of the existing restricting and stifling control practices.

For the students who didn't do as well as they could have, I can't blame them. They have been so conditioned to follow directions, work within guidelines, and repeat what they have been told, that they weren't prepared to *learn*.

I am so used to following set instructions this sort of set me back. I had no idea where to start. This was the first time I had ever received an assignment like this. I then realized if I did it right, I could have fun with this assignment. This was quite an interesting assignment. I would have had more of a learning experience had I thought out the assignment more and planned my time better.

As with the maxim concerning giving a hungry man a fish or teaching him how to fish, schools need to teach students how to learn. Unfortunately, the learning process has too often taken a back seat to the acquisition of content; for it is content that can be measured on standardized tests.

The learning process has too often taken a back seat to the acquisition of content; for it is content that can be measured on standardized tests.

School is for the learning and understanding of new ideas and concepts. In this last project just recently completed, I feel that we as a class not only learned new information, but understood it as well. We learned a great many things, not necessarily on the topic we chose, but on the way we set boundaries for ourselves and how we worked to meet these boundaries. This is the kind of personal understanding about what we as individuals can produce for quality that I feel has fallen short in the school system. ...made us make choices for ourselves that would either make or break our grade. This new-found freedom was troublesome to many, but to others it was a chance to bask in the sunlight.

I was extremely pleased with the students who saw this assignment not just as another meaningless assignment, but as an opportunity to research and learn about a topic AND to learn about learning and how they learn.

Final thoughts

We conducted this unit in the spring. Although not spelled out, by that time, the students had a good idea of what we hoped for in terms of quality and quantity. Given an entire school year, in light of some of the comments and recommendations, I could see a series of preparatory (organizational) assignments leading up to this type of assignment. These introductory assignments would present students with the organizational and research tools that some of them so need. One of these "tools" would be planning or time management.

The last project we did was one we all thought would be easy, we didn't think about the consequences that come with a project with no boundaries. I for one thought this topic would be easy and I didn't think time would be a factor; however it turned out to mean more than I thought it would.

Overall I would enjoy another project similar to this one, I just need to learn to make myself a schedule and follow it strictly. Overall it was fun working on this project. It gave us an opportunity to see how well we can work independently. It also gave us an opportunity to appreciate and understand why teachers harass the students into getting things done.

The only problem with the assignment was the time factor. In general the whole class should have been more prepared.

If I had more time, I would have done better on everything. I feel we should have gone all out in this one to try to learn about something we don't hear about everyday.

I feel we needed more discipline in that area; a jump start to get us going. Journals are the first step on this ladder, although I feel more could be done.

As you put it, we were given "enough rope to hang ourselves," and some of us came pretty close. I would have liked more boundaries and a specific time limit. That way the information would be clearer and there would be enough of it but not too much.

I would recommend that you eliminate ALL guidelines, except the due date. Give your students a full 9 weeks for this, and expect something spectacular. The students would be able to present their material anyway they wished.

Another possibility would be to shorten the time limit and expect less. Yet another possibility would be to set much stricter guidelines.

I think that you should divide the project in half and have us do the model as an assignment and then have us write a report about it or the other way around. I also wish we had more time to work on models that involve a lot of building and workmanship.

The only recommendation that might help this project be more successful is that something should have been passed in every week; this would be so we wouldn't wait until the last minute to complete the project.

I would recommend for the teachers to have us looked at daily and present to us a preferred schedule. Also more time would have been appreciated but with every assignment that is given I can always come up with an excuse for why the due date should be postponed.

Set up a time line, so people won't wait around until the night before. Tell them not to overload themselves with work, to make an outline, and pass it in. Don't just stand around. Get people to work, and don't take any hooey from them. If you do this, people will get better grades and you will be happier.

The next time you do this assignment you should give time designated just to research so they can be sure to find enough information. And if they can't find information they still have time to change projects. Then give them time to do the artifact. If they still don't have enough information it's their fault.

Many of the students, while excited about the initial prospects of academic freedom, were, towards the end of the unit, asking for more guidelines.

If we were to do this again, I would recommend having a guideline sheet listing various manners of presentations. It would help to show some of the many choices that could be made and might inspire some students.

*I think that it was a good idea but you "went wrong" somewhere. Giving us all of this leeway was good, but I think that you gave us **too** much leeway. You should have set more guidelines.*

To look at this entire assignment, I would, even without the above mentioned introductory assignments, repeat this type of activity whenever possible. I believe that the educational benefits and the student motivation greatly outweigh any of the potential drawbacks.

Epilogue

Later in the 1991-92 school year, Ken and I did a similar activity with the same students. Due to the nature of the activity, the topic choices were limited, but we did try to incorporate some student suggestions. Based on a given due date, students developed their own timelines and progress check points, which we monitored. The monitoring was non-graded and consequently non-threatening but did help keep students on schedule. As for reporting methods, since the end of the year was very near, we required students to select two of our usual three reporting methods. This allowed students to eliminate the style with which they were the least comfortable. While the timeline and progress check points did aid in keeping students on schedule, the reporting option didn't significantly improve the final products.

In closing, I'd like to thank students: Josh, Dan, Sarah, Britta, Meredith, Katrina, Lisa, Adam, Adam, Adam, Adam, John, Nick, Peter, Liz, Laurie, Angie, Ben, Steve, Marie, Amanda, Travis, Aaron, and Zach; computer coordinator Judy Chandler, librarian Claudia Mahlman, the administration, and my partner Ken Bonstein. →

10

PUSHING THE ENVELOPE: WHAT CURRICULUM INTEGRATION CAN BE.

Camille Barr

Brown Barge Middle School in Pensacola, Florida provides a curriculum experience for young adolescents that is totally integrated. Separate subject boundaries do not exist and students study streams (themes) based on a central idea or concern they have identified. Brown Barge's bold approach to providing an integrative curriculum is based on sound learning theory and the developmental needs of young adolescents.

The faculty of Brown Barge Middle School is committed to substantive middle grade reform. In an effort to make the middle school experience more important and meaningful, the faculty has begun a process which will improve the delivery of skills and information to students.

Assignments which only ask children to memorize facts and formulae no longer prepare them for the tasks that await them as adults. In this time of rapid change, schools can no longer predict the information and skills students will need in the future. Instead, schools must instill an enthusiasm for learning and teach the skills necessary to locate information pertinent to a problem or job. Traditional curriculum models tend to present knowledge and experiences to students in isolation with little or no perceived usefulness.

Dividing the day into subject-specific lessons remains the approach to presenting the curriculum in most schools. Communicating the practical application of subjects is limited by this design. There may be little attempt to identify student concerns or to include them in what is taught; additionally, the opportunity to solve student and societal problems through creative application and combination of a diverse range of knowledge areas is almost nonexistent.

Changing to meet the challenge

Brown Barge Middle School, as originally conceived by the school board, was given the challenge of implementing changes which address the curriculum issues mentioned above. New ideas have been undertaken in response to this mandate—team teaching, interdisciplinary units, theme-focused instruction,

99

cross-level teaching, flexible scheduling, computer aided lessons, alternative evaluation methods, and extensive enrichment classes called "discoveries" or "seminars."

About the school...

Escambia County is situated in the panhandle of Florida on the Gulf of Mexico in a combined rural and urban setting. It covers 661 square miles and has a population of 267,000 people, ranks 13th in Florida and 86th in the nation in student population. In a district of 44,000 students, the total middle school population is 9,500 students. Brown Barge, a magnet middle school of 500 with students in grades 6-8, is one of 10 middle schools in this district.

The student population includes the following: 20% who meet district criteria for students at risk; 33% who are identified gifted, one third of whom are at risk; and 30% who qualify for free or reduced lunch. The ethnic distribution of Brown Barge is 66% white, 28% black, and 5% other minorities, consistent to the ethnic distribution throughout Escambia County.

Changing to meet the challenge

The curriculum development process suggested by James Beane in *The Middle School Curriculum: From Rhetoric to Reality* (1990a), begins with a survey of student and parents concerning skills and information appropriate to middle level education. Students were also surveyed to determine what concerns they had about themselves, the world in which they live, and what they considered to be important in their education. The result of this process was the development of a new curriculum responsive to these concerns, which will assist in preparing students for their futures.

The success of these changes, a study of the research, the parent/student survey results, the call for educational reform, and curriculum conversations with middle school leaders across the country led to identifying the following components of a challenging middle school curriculum:
1. A continuous and systematic identification of the concerns of middle school students, parents, and teachers.
2. Use of these concerns as the core of "curriculum streams" which challenge the student to apply knowledge areas creatively.
3. The extensive application of appropriate technology.
4. The involvement of teams of teachers in writing and implementing curriculum.
5. Three tiers of instruction which provide for compensatory instruction, acquiring knowledge pertinent to student concerns, and a practical context in which to creatively apply that knowledge.

6. An evaluation, collaborative learning profile which includes parent/ teacher/student dialogue.

Our vision of middle level curriculum reflects a concern for the needs and interests of young adolescents and the world in which they live. This vision suggests that what students need to know stems from questions they have about themselves, their world, and challenges the world poses for them. We believe this curriculum addresses these questions and challenges. In the next section, we explain the key components for our new curriculum, which is THE curriculum for the entire school.

What students need to know stems from questions they have about themselves, their world, and challenges the world poses for them.

Our plan and how it works

At Brown Barge Middle School the school year is divided into nine week quarters. Each quarter students register for one stream, a thematic unit of study based on a central idea or concern identified by students. Stream topics (themes) are inferred from the results of periodic surveys of students, parents, and faculty. These surveys provide responses concerning personal, societal and educational issues. Student journals provide other opportunities for students to suggest stream topics.

The stream premise, an assertive statement about the importance of the stream topic, provides focus for the quarter. The premise should be validated by the activities and knowledge areas contained within the stream. The premise is most apparent to the student in the Simulation Tier, but its presence motivates and provides meaning in all tiers.

Carefully constructed streams necessitate and motivate student mastery of specific portions of academic disciplines and allow students to see themselves as "players" in resolving issues contained in each stream.

Prior to registration, each student receives the course offerings which included title, topic, premise, and description for each stream. During the first week of each nine week stream, students are given (1) a rationale for the overall stream topic, (2) application, content, activities, and products, (3) simulations and products, (4) student evaluation criteria, and (5) a description of the technology involved and how it is to be used. See Figure 1 for an example of a stream description.

Figure 1

TOPIC: Dwellings

TITLE: Give Me Shelter

STREAM PREMISE: The diversity of man is reflected in the dwellings in which he lives.

STREAM DESCRIPTION: Through a combination of academic inquiry and hands-on building and drawing, students learn that the diversity of man is reflected in the dwellings in which he lives. In this stream, students discover how climate, culture, history, geography and natural resources have combined to determine the houses man has built. Students engage in writing activities that include journal entries, letters, reports and short stories. Technology enhances research, oral and visual presentations, and displays. Students also develop math and geometry skills by working with perspective drawing, architectural drafting and financing the construction of a home.

As a stream progresses and is evaluated by the students and teachers, student concerns will continue to be a part of the stream writing and evaluation process. These concerns will be used to change existing streams when called for and to create new ones. Valuing student opinion communicates a message of self worth and an ability to effect change. When students are encouraged to express their opinions with confidence, they are provided "practice" for the civic needs, and the opportunity to lead productive adult lives is established.

Three tier instruction

The Three Tier System of instruction which includes *Acquisition, Application,* and *Simulation* provides the structure necessary to deliver this approach to learning. Each stream requires learning and using knowledge and skills.

Acquisition: The Acquisition Tier provides the student with most of the basic skills necessary for success in this curriculum. Anticipated areas of skills study would include math, writing, reading, and social skills. The precise composition of this tier is dependent upon the characteristics of the school population. For example, before acquisition instruction in mathematics, writing, and reading can begin, certain student populations might require instruction in affective areas (constructive peer interaction, conflict resolution, etc.) so that the social skills necessary to succeed are in place. Student history and diagnostic tests are used to determine which affective or academic areas a student needs to address.

The amount of time that each student devotes to acquisition activities is based on need as determined by student history and diagnostic tests. When possible, acquisition instruction should be computer-driven, which allows heterogeneous grouping with regard to content and level of mastery.

Creative problem solving, study skills, effective group interaction, and computer literacy are also skills which a student must possess in order to participate fully in any stream. These skills are imparted and augmented as a natural consequence of participation in an integrated curriculum. They are also reflective of the tasks and environment in the contemporary work place. Development of these skills is an advantage of this curriculum design.

Application: The Application Tier consists of the presentation of knowledge areas which support the stream. Each stream demands varying degrees of involvement from social sciences, language arts, higher mathematics, natural sciences, visual arts, performing arts, and foreign language as well as any other identifiable knowledge area. The instruction at this tier employs a variety of teaching strategies including, but not limited to, computer-driven instruction, independent learning, cooperative learning, peer teaching, research, and multimedia instruction. A student's interest at the Application Tier could lie beyond the scope of the stream. This opportunity for "student enrichment" is most easily accommodated at this tier of the curriculum. The amount of time spent at The Application Tier varies with the degree of preparation needed for simulations. Relevance of the application content to the simulations and stream premise must be established at the Application Tier in order to maintain student enthusiasm.

Simulation: The simulation brings all of the preparation gained at the Acquisition and Application Tiers to bear on the central issue or concern of the stream and creatively applies that knowledge to those issues and concerns. Results of the simulation could be confined to the school environment or could impact the community at large. Activities and products of a simulation vary with the subject of the stream and with the way a team of teachers chooses to approach it. For example, a stream addressing global hunger could result in a wide variety of products including the production of a pertinent play, TV or radio show, evaluation of botanical experiments, greenhouse design and construction, mural contrasting feast and famine, documentary on the politics of hunger, or role playing arbitration of a geopolitical cause of hunger.

The Simulation Tier of the curriculum is best explained by example, but a few criteria for maintaining student enthusiasm can be articulated. Opportunities for synthesis, analysis, and evaluation of products should be present (higher level thinking skills). Simulations should impact or have implications beyond the school setting. Opportunity should exist for students to express their ideas in ways that parallel the civic and social processes they will encounter as adults.

Simulations should have implications beyond the school setting. Opportunity should exist for students to express ideas in ways that parallel the civic and social processes of adults.

Integrating technology

Technology should be viewed by the student as an implicit part of the curriculum. Perception of the computer and peripherals as devices to be used on special assignments or as reward for completion of regular assignments is replaced by a perception of utility and continuous access. A student orientation stream and a teacher training component provide the instruction necessary to use the technology.

A high technological profile (interactive video, computerized instruction, database access, etc.) at the Acquisition Tier facilitates efficient delivery of essential basic skills and automates prescriptive and record keeping tasks. The use of sophisticated technology to deliver acquisition instruction also validates the importance of the work for the student and provides motivation.

The Application Tier makes use of a broad range of technological devices and services. When students and teachers are able to use this technology—laser disk players, video cameras and recorders, video editing and digitizing hardware, CD ROM drives, large screen monitors, and closed circuit television—the delivery of the Application Tier becomes a process which emphasizes discovery rather than drill and memorization.

Simulations incorporate technology to varying degrees according to their design. Construction of a space colony would utilize computer-aided design software, telecommunications capabilities, local data base access, and tools to build a model. The production of a documentary video would likely entail technical capabilities from video editing to computer generation of graphics and animation.

Technology should be employed in accordance with the nature of the task and not employed for its own sake.

Instructional rationales for use of technology include motivation of the students, expedition of the learning process, inclusion of multisensory learning, and expansion of the possibilities for student assignments and projects. Technology should be employed in accordance with the nature of the task and not employed for its own sake.

Student and teacher roles in integrative curriculum

The teaching role, demanded by an integrative and largely technologically delivered curriculum, requires additional professional training of most middle grade faculties. The integrated approach at Brown Barge assumes autonomous teaching teams to implement a curriculum that is driven by thematic interpretation of student concerns. Many middle grade teachers have experience with a "teaming" concept in which there is contribution from each subject area in an "interdisciplinary" context. Useful as this preparation may be, the degree of collaboration required of a faculty committed to a truly integrative approach (elimination of accepted subject area boundaries with student concerns determining methodology and content) is much greater. Teachers' avocational interests, facilitative skills, enthusiasm for learning, and capacity for professional cooperation will routinely supplant "certification area" preparation in an integrative curriculum.

The degree of collaboration required of a faculty committed to a truly integrative approach is much greater.

Through participation in curriculum restructuring, teachers become familiar with, if not trained for, an "integrative teaching role." A faculty intent on full integration of its curriculum must engage in what can be aptly termed a cathartic process. Methodical rejection of professional axioms which have defined the content areas and teacher role is central to this process. The philosophy, which mandates these redefinitions, as well as the streams which implement it, should be articulated by the faculty. This demanding task addresses every nuance of the implementation of an integrative curriculum. The new teaching role is revealed, as well as defined, by the teachers taking part in the restructuring process.

Student activities in an integrative environment consist primarily of cooperative or individual tasks involving research, document or presentation preparation, concrete manipulation, and product evaluation. Content is largely experiential in nature or dependent upon student discovery. The volume of information encompassed by an integrative topic requires the teacher to guide the student to appropriate information rather than attempt to impart the entire scope of the topic. These circumstances demand an active and enthusiastic student. Effective teaching will become facilitative.

Evaluation process—the collaborative learning profile

The Collaborative Learning Profile (CLP) includes a portfolio of student work, student journal entries, teacher evaluation of student performance, test results, parental input, and CLP conferences.

The portfolio consists of examples of the entire spectrum of student products from three-dimensional models to electronically stored writing projects. Examples include video, three-dimensional projects or photo evidence of the projects, records of group presentations, performances, records of community services performed, and any other student assignments completed in conjunction with the stream.

Students are given time to submit regularly scheduled journal entries during a stream. Dated journal entries recount all assignments undertaken since the last entry and provide the student an opportunity to reflect upon the stream content. Student suggestions for stream improvement and new stream topics are encouraged. Teachers involved in each stream are responsible for a group of students and respond to student concern in the individual journals.

Teacher evaluation of student performance is an important part of the CLP. Teaching teams compile a process-oriented evaluation for each student in their stream. As a stream progresses, each teacher regularly assigns appropriate marks to all students in twenty process-oriented criteria. Examples of the criteria used include the following: shares information, interacts constructively and congenially, communicates ideas effectively, writes persuasively, conducts meaningful research, manages time wisely, and follows through on assigned tasks. The use of product-oriented criteria focuses on the end of the learning experience and ignores the integral processes. The use of process-oriented criteria allows a closer examination of the entire learning experience and examines factors that enable, or prevent, a student from performing effectively.

The use of process-oriented criteria allows a closer examination of the entire learning experience and examines factors that affect a student's performance.

Test results derived from diagnostic tests, nationally normed tests, and from teacher generated tests satisfy parental demand for an indication of content comprehension and retention, as well as teacher need for prescriptive data.

Parental input is important to the success of an integrative curriculum. Parent comments, questions, and criticisms are solicited via the student journal and during the CLP conferences. Frequent parental review of the student journal provides (by modem when feasible) an additional avenue for monitoring student progress.

The Collaborative Learning Profile (CLP) encompasses a broad range of review techniques. Students should regard the CLP as a regularly occurring opportunity to review their accomplishments with parents and teachers. Looking at many parts of the "learning process" offers more opportunities for praise and will also increase the effectiveness of instruction.

Meeting our goals

The curricular changes at Brown Barge Middle School are sweeping and have broad implications beyond the school setting, in colleges of education, state legislatures, and departments of education. However, it should be noted that these changes are within the bounds of current professional theory. The Brown Barge faculty is involved in a concerted effort to effect substantive curriculum reform. The Brown Barge administration has actively sought the counsel of nationally recognized middle school educators, theorists, and academicians in order to stimulate this reform. Information has been made available to the faculty by means of professional travel, faculty reports, on-site workshops, and professional literature. This curriculum design is the result of these efforts. It employs what the faculty considers to be the best individual components from the spectrum of current middle grade philosophy. →

III

Dissolving Boundaries: Strategies and Reflections

It is easier to move a cemetery than to affect a change
in curriculum.
                                    —Woodrow Wilson

Things don't happen, they are made to happen. And
in the field of education, they are made to happen by
you.
                                    —John F. Kennedy

11 | THE CURRICULUM PLANNING PROCESS: MORE THAN INTERDISCIPLINARY UNITS...

Planning integrative curriculum is not inherently difficult, but as we have noted throughout this book, it assumes new ways of thinking about what is important, and it certainly challenges many well-ingrained "regularities" of schools. While nearly every prospective teacher takes a course in curriculum as an undergraduate and perhaps again as a graduate student, the process as outlined in college courses and in curriculum textbooks seems remote from the actual practice of curriculum planning and development as it occurs in good middle schools.

In this chapter we discuss a practical, useable process of curriculum planning which will assist teams and individual teachers in moving along the curriculum continuum. Please note that this process does not short-circuit essential elements of curriculum planning, in fact it is based on those fundamental components and seeks to extend the process in a clearer manner. While hardly new, the curriculum planning process we describe assists teachers in moving from a traditional to a more fully integrative curriculum.

Although many interdisciplinary unit planning models exist, they provide a template for writing discrete units, but NOT for carrying them out. And as the curriculum continuum suggests, the interdisciplinary unit may not be regarded by teachers as a serious part of the larger curriculum. Interdisciplinary units are simply way-stations for teams discovering more fully integrative models to answer the essential curriculum question, "What do young adolescents need to know and be able to do?"

Gordon Vars (1993) provides a very useful description of the unit planning process in his "15 Steps in Planning an Interdisciplinary Unit." Chris

111

Stevenson and Judy Carr (1993) go a step beyond that in their "Integrated Studies Planning Framework." Both of these frameworks assist the curriculum planner in developing units which have a focus and a specific plan.

Developing an interdisciplinary unit should not be an end in itself; rather it is a means to allow teachers to take first steps toward true integration.

Likewise, our Integrative Curriculum Planning Process allows teachers to move across the Curriculum Continuum. Interdisciplinary, integrated, and integrative units should be flexible, easily adapted resource plans; developing an interdisciplinary unit, for example, should not be viewed as an end in itself; rather, it is a means to allow curriculum planners to take those first steps toward true integration. We believe our process allows for the full range of integrative curriculum planning, moving well beyond interdisciplinary unit development.

Asking the "right" questions

Before we look further at the curriculum planning process and how it works, a series of questions must be carefully considered before any attempts are made to "restructure" the **current** middle level curriculum. **Curriculum change is difficult because it is highly personal. It requires a fundamental shift in individual beliefs about what the curriculum should be and how it can best be experienced. Therefore, any attempts at altering present curriculum must involve an intensive examination of a number of fundamentally held beliefs before something new can be explored.**

The following questions must be posed and answered by all involved in curriculum planning:

1. What is the purpose of the middle level curriculum? Should students study a limited number of disciplines or topics in-depth or should they explore a general curriculum which allows investigation of many areas? At what point is it necessary to focus the curriculum on discipline specialization? What should the general curriculum look like? What beliefs drive practices?

2. What skills, knowledge, competencies, and attitudes should receive priority? With new job skills required of workers, a national debate over standards, and much discussion about what constitutes an educated person, studying this question is mandatory. Since we can't do everything, what should we do?

3. Are some subjects or areas of study more important than others? If so, what are they? Should some areas of study receive priority in scheduling or time allotted? Does the organization reflect the purpose of the curriculum or is it made to fit existing structures?

4 What should the learning outcomes of middle level education be? To what extent should the curriculum be coordinated with other teachers? To what degree should the curriculum reflect the expectations of the high school? To what extent should the curriculum reflect the present needs of students? Is there a core of skills, knowledge, competencies, and attitudes that must be learned by all? Should the curriculum be designed to create new knowledge as well as disseminate old information? With the varied calls for new standards, what should they be?

5. Who should determine the curriculum? What is the role of the federal government, state legislature, school committee, other special interest groups, teachers, and students in determining the curriculum? More specifically, as major stakeholders, how do we define the roles of teachers and students in this process? Whose curriculum is it?

6. Should we have different curricula for students with different interests and aspirations? Who will determine which curriculum is appropriate for students? Are there some experiences all students should have? How can the curriculum promote higher aspirations?

7. How should learning be organized? What is the best way for students to learn? Should we continue to separate subjects as we have traditionally done? Should we blur subject lines and correlate disciplines where possible? Or, should we provide an integrative approach?

8. What are the philosophical bases for the curriculum? Is it based on the developmental needs of the learner, cultural needs of a group, sequenced content of a discipline; or is it a combination of individual and societal needs?

9. Shall everyone have access to the same curriculum? Should all students have opportunities to learn the same curriculum? How do we ensure equity and advancement for all ability levels?

10. How will we measure worthwhile learning? New definitions of learning require new assessment structures. How do we blend traditional strategies with new, authentic assessment strategies to provide students and the public with accountability? How do we change the reliance on standardized tests for letting parents know the degree to which students are learning? How do we measure new forms of learning—collaboration, student reflections, self-esteem, projects, and other types of learning that do not lend themselves to paper and pencil measures?

11. What beliefs do teachers hold about how much can be learned and who can learn? Can all students be held to high expectations? Is success in school due more to one's ability or one's effort? Is ability alterable?

12. Who is responsible for student learning? Is the teacher or the student responsible for student success; or, more importantly, what is the role of each? Key beliefs about efficacy and responsibility must be explored. How do these relate to curriculum determination?

13. Who should be active participants in the learning process? Should students make significant decisions about their education? What is the role of parents in the curriculum process? With all the special interest groups competing for curriculum space, how do you determine who gets heard and who gets results?

14. Are there some subjects which integrate more easily? Should some subjects be taught separately? Should the curriculum determine the organization?

15. Are there some individuals who cannot be successful in school? Who are they and when do we know that? Is there a quota on smart people or is it possible for everyone to be smart? Is intelligence narrowly defined or are there multiple intelligences. What types of intelligences get rewarded? Is there a limit on the types and amounts of rewards that can be received?

16. Are there some teachers for whom integrated curriculum will not work? Are some teachers too inflexible to change to new ways of presenting curriculum and instruction? Are some teachers effective only in a more conventionally organized class? Are there instances of schools where it is easier to work alone than to work with reluctant colleagues?

The curriculum planning process

While it is important to see and read about other schools, it has never been possible to transport or fully adopt someone else's curriculum without fundamental changes.

These questions presuppose that the process of "discovering" the answers will tell much about the curriculum itself. No answers are assumed and no answers are taken for granted. Most importantly, the answers to these and similar questions are personal and the act of discovering them determines the curriculum. While it is important to see, experience, and read about other schools and their successes, it has never been possible to transport or fully adopt someone else's curriculum without fundamental changes. Schools trying to do so find themselves in difficulty because they can adopt the organizational aspects of the curriculum—a block schedule, interdisciplinary teams and similar structures—but because they have short-circuited the personal, and ultimately meaningful work of seeking answers to **their** questions, they have not completed the process.

Contrary to school practice and public perception, curriculum planning is continuous, and should occur in many forms and at various times during the year. In spite of the proclivity for schools to consider curriculum planning as a tangential, summer activity where teachers are paid to "write" curriculum, often a curious process of copying the table of contents of textbooks, authentic curriculum planning is more thoughtful and more rigorous.

The type of responsive curricula which Arnold, Toepfer, Stevenson, Beane, and others (Dickinson, 1993) advocate comes through intense and often contentious work in trying to answer the questions stated previously. While most teachers have participated in curriculum work of a traditional type, far fewer teachers have had the opportunity to grapple with the key questions we have described. Stated simply, neither the expectation nor the opportunities for curriculum exploration exist in most schools. Underlying these lack of opportunities, perhaps, is the notion that curriculum is "handed down" by experts, not those closest to it, the teachers and students. Yet, curriculum development is fundamentally a human enterprise, not a technical one. When all is said and done, the most important factor is the human interaction and communication, the people who are affected. Not surprisingly, curriculum planning should involve teachers in the very same process of critical thinking, problem-solution, analysis, reflection, and evaluation that teachers wish to teach their students. Unfortunately rarely do students see the teacher as a self-directed learner.

Curriculum development is fundamentally a human enterprise, not a technical one.

And yet, the teacher's role in curriculum improvement is essential. Teachers make hundreds of decisions a day, most about curriculum. For example, deciding what instructional materials to use or what type of emphasis to place on certain ideas recognizes the curriculum influence. In addition, when teachers group students, encourage them to ask and answer certain types of questions, or select from a variety of learning activities, these are all curriculum decisions. It is also important to guard against minimizing the role of the teacher in an integrative curricular setting. Comments like, "the teacher is a facilititator" or "the teacher guides and rarely teaches" fail to understand the essential role of the teacher. While teachers as lecturers and dispensers of information will disappear, teachers will now have time to truly teach!

The role of young adolescents will change drastically as they become more active participants in the curriculum planning process.

The role of young adolescents will also change drastically as they become more active participants in the curriculum planning process. Instead of being the passive recipient of the curriculum, students will be asked to make decisions about the curriculum. The key here is the recognition that without their involvement, students will have little engagement or interest in what happens in school. While Beane's Integrative Curriculum proposal is dramatic in its depth of student involvement, many other curriculum planning strategies include student involvement at lesser, but nonetheless essential levels. Student decision-making in selecting activities in interdisciplinary units, deciding on materials to use in achieving a particular goal, deciding with whom to work, and deciding on ways to evaluate and assess one's work are all examples of the types of decisions students should make.

Student involvement in the curriculum will proceed positively as students become more comfortable. As they learn to trust their involvement, they will push for more and more voice in the curriculum. While this is exactly what we want for teachers, to move out of the traditional "teacher does everything" mode, it will not be easy or painless.

Students are often unwilling to accept responsibility for the thinking required when making decisions about curriculum. We should not be surprised by this, for when placed in a conventional classroom where the teacher does all the real work, and makes all the decisions, students **are** comfortable in their passive roles. *(That is your job! Just tell us what you want us to do!)* Teachers must be willing to take time necessary to alter this attitude and not give up when students rebel against their new role. After all, it is no wonder that students feel comfortable in their traditional role; they have had many years of experience learning it by being told that in schools they react, not act!

Young adolescents display an extremely high level of achievement when they work on projects which incorporate personal interests and use skills and knowledge they possess.

Young adolescents have wonderful ideas, are interested in a great many things, and have the skills necessary to pursue ideas to a high level. We rarely give them credit for what they can do and we don't expect them to do nearly enough! Young adolescents display an extremely high level of achievement when they have opportunities to work on projects which incorporate personal areas of interest and use skills and knowledge they possess. In conjunction with the Middle Level Curriculum Project (McDonough,1991), young adolescent students were asked to respond to an 11 item survey designed to elicit from youngsters possible curriculum themes. McDonough, one of the authors/researchers, responds, "Reading the responses reveals the breadth and depth of student experiences. It reinforces the need to ask young adolescents directly what are their concerns and questions. Most young adolescents revealed deep concerns about certain issues as well as frustrations about which few, if any, adults are aware" (p.32).

I wish I knew why the world has so many problems and why the different countries just can't get along with each other. I wish I knew why people treat the earth the way they do, spraying aerosols into the atmosphere, ruining the ozone burning trash, filling landfills, using up all our natural resources

I wish I knew how to be a better friend. I find myself in many different kinds of cliques and wondering why I can't hold onto one.

I wish I knew more about religion. I'm Catholic and
I'm supposed to believe that God is going to save us all, but
then I start thinking about the Buddhists. What if they are
right and and I am wrong?

We can't afford to ignore the powerful and compelling interests and motivation that young adolescents have for learning. One of the great unanswered questions is why students lose their love of learning, at least in school, at such a young age. Does this happen when we focus too much on teaching rather than learning?

Do students lose their love of learning because we focus too much on teaching rather than learning?

Student involvement in curriculum planning at the classroom level, or any other level, has been minimal at best, usually consisting of limited choices of activities which have already been selected by their teachers. While interdisciplinary units and integrated units may allow students to participate more fully, even in these types of activities, student involvement is often little more than selecting from teacher-produced activities. Rarely do students actually participate in the planning process of such a curriculum.

In our own work with young adolescents, we have seen genuine engagement, interest, and motivation for learning when that learning has meaning for them. One of the joys of teaching this age group is their wide-ranging, ever-changing interests, as well as their ability for becoming interested in almost anything with mimimal levels of teacher encouragement. That is certainly one of the secrets of middle level teaching as well.

As noted earlier, Beane includes student input as the core of the curriculum planning process. "In an integrative approach, where the questions and concerns of young people are taken seriously, the planning begins by asking them to say what those questions and concerns are and subsequently what themes they cluster around" (Beane, 1993a).

Teachers who have never engaged in this type of activity with young adolescents find it both exhilarating and frightening. It certainly places the teacher in a different role, a role where power and control is shared equally with students. For many, it is a shock. At the same time, it illustrates very clearly the "positive possibilities" as Peter Scales (1991) would say, of our youth. For it shows how interested they are in important ideas, how sensitive they are to their own needs as well as those around them, and finally, how excited about learning they are if we take away artificial barriers.

Arnold (1993) takes another tack as he argues forcefully for an empowering curriculum, built on a positive view of students, which "...helps them understand how society shapes their development and at times exploits them."

No doubt there are many ways to explore this aspect of empowerment through curriculum. The most feasible way that occurs to me is through a study of adolescence itself, confronting the societal forces which influence early adolescent development in the process (p. 9).

Like the curriculum planning process which focuses on students, the empowering curriculum requires young adolescents to participate at the highest level with ideas and concepts which have great import to them, as well as the world around them.

Local control is everything

Glatthorn (1987) suggests several different types of curricula from the formal, to the tested, to the taught, to the assessed. While it is a helpful concept to think in terms of the influence that different curricula have on teaching and learning, for too long there has been an over-dependence on external influences—textbooks, state and federal curriculum guidelines, and, especially, tests. Simply put, teachers and students have not had enough influence on changing and improving the curriculum. The myth of the curriculum "expert" is still very much a part of us, and that expert is almost always someone from somewhere else, rather than experts in our own schools and communities.

> **The myth of the curriculum "expert" is still very much a part of us, and that expert is almost always someone from somewhere else.**

Just as students are finding their voices, so too are teachers who realize that the curriculum is ultimately an issue of local control. In many schools, the real curriculum, or what Glatthorn would call the "taught" curriculum, is designated by teachers. Given the myriad suggestions for what curriculum should be and what materials and activities should be used, the classroom teacher still maintains much control in deciding what to do, how long to do it, what materials to use, and what "slant" to give content and skills. Those key decisions certainly constitute real local control.

Unfortunately, the difficulty about who controls the curriculum lies more with perception than fact. Even though teachers inherently have power over the curriculum, they THINK that someone else actually controls it. And, thus the possibilities for improvement are limited when one thinks that no individual teacher has the authority to make changes in the curriculum. In too many cases, therefore, the question about changing the curriculum—"what should the curriculum be,"—is rarely posed.

THE INTEGRATIVE CURRICULUM PLANNING PROCESS

Once a group of teachers have reached consensus on answers to the questions posed earlier, those common understandings and shared beliefs provide the philosophical underpinnings for actually planning an integrative experience. The planning process for such an experience includes a number of considerations divided into three categories: 1) selecting a "unit" of study, 2) selecting learning activities, and 3) assessing the unit and the planning process.

Corbett and Blum (1993), and Arnold (1985) remind us of the critical importance of local planning and the best thoughts of teacher experts. This curriculum planning process is hardly a cut and dried affair; rather, it is a dynamic, ever-changing process which does not resemble typical curriculum guides or lesson plans, and thus might be difficult to imagine.

1. Selecting a unit of study

Integrative units must be developed from a conceptual framework that is justifiable, developmentally appropriate, and philosophically defensible. Teachers must understand the philosophical and conceptual framework that permits them to do what they know is best for young adolescents.

Units of study selected on the basis of teacher interest one time, student interest the next, local interests, or units taught simply because they "worked last year" do not have a conceptual framework that withstands such examination. To randomly select themes ensures that the unit will be envisioned from the beginning as outside the personal curriculum and will have little philosophical or practical legitimacy. Many well-intentioned interdisciplinary units fail to reach their potential because they are completely teacher-selected.

Student-teacher planning: Beane (1993b) describes a curriculum planning process in which students and teachers propose topics for study based on personal concerns of young adolescents and the common issues they currently face and will face in society. If present interests of students, reflecting their developmental needs, are aligned with critical issues in our society (i.e., environmental survival, learning to live with others), learning will be practical, meaningful, and engaging. All units should emphasize the concepts of democracy, human dignity, and cultural diversity.

Probably the most contentious aspect of integrative curriculum for many teachers is allowing students to participate in the planning. Teachers are not accustomed to sharing power and students initially resist having to "do so much work." Yet, it makes sense that when there is ownership of the curriculum, students enjoy learning. When students look for answers to their own questions, it

Student involvement in curriculum planning is the most important component if middle level curriculum is to become more integrated.

provides a training ground for later success. While we don't wish to overstate this issue, student involvement in curriculum planning is the most important component if middle level curriculum is to become more integrated and truly meet the needs of young adolescents.

There are many fine examples of successful units in which students have explored their own questions. Significantly, the notion of a student-influenced curriculum does not imply that whatever students want to do is acceptable. Nor does it assume that the curriculum is student-directed, with little teacher involvement. It does reflect a belief that students and their interests, needs, issues, and questions should be a major force in shaping what and how they learn, with the conceptual and philosophical framework determined by educators.

Collaborative student-teacher planning must become the focus for the middle level curriculum. It is important to note, that this type of student-teacher planning is critical to the engagement of individual students, and follows the curriculum work that teachers and other adults have completed previously. That is to say, teachers must first answer the question, *What should the middle level curriculum be?* before opening up that question to students.

Goals for the unit: If students and teachers plan collaboratively, then it follows that they should share a common set of goals for the unit planned. As a part of the shared curriculum planning process, students and teachers decide what will constitute a knowledgeable person at the completion of the unit. A "backwards planning" process is used to narrow what we want young adolescents to learn about, from and during the unit. Such outcomes then become the "road-map" for the rest of the unit. Stevenson and Carr (1993) suggest focusing on a culminating event for your activity. "Establishing a culmination ensures that the unit will in fact end..." and "a culminating event also contributes focus to a study and enhances everyone's sense of accomplishment when it is completed."

The goals for any unit must include those developed cooperatively between students and teachers, but should also include those goals which are teacher selected. They should be clearly focused, succinctly stated, and understood by all involved in the study. As such, the goals should be returned to frequently to ensure that all are working toward the same ends.

Problem focus: Success in school, as in the world, requires abilities to effectively identify and solve problems. Thematic units must be experiences in inquiry, not merely subject or topic units—*Pilgrims, dinosaurs, sports.* Since the process which Beane recommends includes a heavy emphasis on answering student posed questions about their own lives, students will study, explore, and create knowledge around issues that are real in today's world and that need solutions. Such curriculum themes as *transitions, identities, commercialism,* and *caring* are excellent examples of units which require a problem focus

Relationship to the existing curriculum: One of the concerns of teachers who contemplate integrative curriculum is that all of the content that they feel comfortable teaching will disappear. This is not true. As Beane notes (1993), we are talking about re-positioning the content and the skills of the conventional curriculum, not doing away with it!

For those who are encouraged to stay close to the official curriculum of the district, it is possible to begin to move toward more integrative curriculum AND correlate that with the conventional curriculum. Reference should be made to the skills, knowledge, and content the unit is attempting to address; it is relatively easy to track the pieces of the official curriculum in integrative units.

As teachers feel more comfortable in "challenging" the conventional curriculum, they will inevitably investigate the "regularities" of it and begin to ask, "why" or "why not"? Why is topic A included and not topics B,C, and D? Why can't we spend four weeks on Latin America instead of only two weeks? This process of questionning is especially positive because if forces us to consider possibilities we have not considered before.

2. Selecting activities and planning for the unit

This is the fun part of the unit and a place in which teachers (and students) are most creative. After deciding on the direction which the integrative study will take, specific details of the activities must be given. During the initial activity, when students came to a consensus on the topic(s) they wished to study, they also brainstormed possible activities to be included in such a unit. Now, it is up to the teachers to put those activities into some sort of a meaningful whole by setting a timeline, by adding to a well-rounded set of activities, and by planning a variety of activities to complement students' learning styles. This is where the teachers' knowledge of curriculum is particularly helpful, as they provide balance to the content and skills previously suggested by students as worthy of study.

The activities should be described and categorized according to type: initial, on-going, culminating, and evaluative. Particular attention should be given to evaluative activities that are located throughout the unit and require students to exhibit responsibility as well as demonstrate accountability for their own learning. These need to be of many types, with particular emphasis on authentic assessment devices, demonstrations, portfolios, and the like. Student journal writing with specific reflections on their work as well as varied opportunities to think deeply about their work are critical pieces of student learning.

Skill development is more important here than in conventional curricula because students must, "be skilled, not just have skills" (Arnold,1985). And, it is much more challenging for the teacher to weave in skill development lessons when the skill is needed, rather than at some indiscriminate point during the year. On the other hand, skill work is much more immediate and the rewards for demonstrating skill in reading, writing, computing, and other skills is more reinforcing than in traditional classrooms.

The integrative unit plan is really a resource of possible activities from which students and teachers may choose.

Because all units and groups of students and adults are different, deciding on how long to continue units is problematic. Units should last as long as everyone is engaged and continues to show interest, whether that is two weeks with one group or eight weeks with another. Because integrative curriculum demands flexibility in teaching, as students constantly change directions and discover new learnings, the integrative unit plan is really a resource of possible activities, from which students and teachers may choose. Over several years, the list of activities will grow dramatically, and while every activity will not be used each year, the large list should also allow students to pursue individual projects. This is an important consideration; because even though the topic was suggested by the class, not all students will have an equal interest in it.

An action plan with timeline included serves as the blueprint for the unit. Carefully constructed, it serves as the larger plan for teachers and students and should describe in detail the activities, deadlines, responsibilities, and other information crucial to the plan. Because such an integrative unit most often includes work and study in the community, information about these resources should also be included.

3. Assessing, evaluating, and documenting the process

Just as a variety of assessment activities are built in for students as they progress in their integrative studies, so too must we continually assess the **process** of integrative curriculum. Not only is assessment important as a barometer and gauge of where we have been and where we want to go, given the stranglehold which conventional curriculum has on schools, it is doubly important to show if integrative curriculum has been successful.

Teachers have used alternatives to paper and pencil asessments in their classrooms for a long time. Projects, plays, demonstrations and exhibitions have always been part of an effective teacher's repertoire of teaching strategies. Most of us can remember in junior high school creating a project in science or social studies—models, posters, working with a group of students to produce a literacy magazine, or building a chest of drawers in industrial arts from a set of blueprints.

What is different today is that these activities are now referred to as authentic assessments and in many instances replace pencil and paper tests. In the past, these projects were viewed only as activities rather than as assessments of learning. They were recognized as worthwhile projects but not scientific, academic or measurable examples to be related to an all-important grade.

Schools included in this book are part of the movement to change this outdated, obsolete, and harmful way of narrowly looking at how we measure student learning. These schools don't see projects as just projects. They see them as vital pieces to complete the assessment profile. They don't see exhibitions just as artifacts that fill the gym at the annual curriculum fair. Instead of the teacher separating subjects, skills, and knowledge into distinct components and then creating items to estimate mastery, teachers are beginning to require students to develop artifacts, portfolios, and projects that allow them to integrate subjects, skills, and knowledge areas into a whole from which the teacher and students can identify component learning if needed. In other words, instead of narrowly measuring skill identification or knowledge recognition, teachers now require students to apply skills and knowledge by demonstrating competency or by producing an artifact that illustrates understanding.

Teachers require students to apply skills and knowledge by demonstrating competency or by producing an artifact that illustrates understanding.

Assessing the process is important. As several of these seven schools have written, determining what is happening and how it is going, is a formative not a summative activity. Assessing beliefs, reflecting on the success of unit planning, or determining the successes and failures of the unit are key aspects of curriculum development. Data are needed to assist in reflection, decision-making, public awareness, and documentation of success and growth. Formative assessment becomes a mindset. In many respects, it drives the change process and provides the rationale for continued exploration. Remember, the new curriculum for the students is also the new curriculum for teachers. To assess only how students are doing with this change and not those who are primarily responsible for this change is to guarantee a quick return to the old curriculum. Both stakeholders deserve this attention. →

12 REFLECTIONS—WHAT WE HAVE LEARNED FROM THESE SCHOOLS

What have we learned from the excellent work of teachers and students who have been engaged in curriculum integration projects, particularly in these seven middle level schools? After reading the curriculum stories, themes and generalizations rise to the top. And the contradictions, ambiguities, and the sometimes "hunches more than facts" that characterize the "lessons" of such work are apparent.

As more individuals and teams of teachers attempt this kind of work and reflect on what they have found, the more we will know about what really works. Why, for example, do two different schools take the same approach on an issue, like curriculum integration, and end up with such widely disparate outcomes?

The work of teachers in these seven schools is significant and deserves our attention. In the past five years curriculum has finally become an important issue, but there are still too few schools making serious attempts at improving their curriculum. Fortunately, these seven schools provide valuable experiences, knowledge, and guidance for others working toward an integrated curriculum.

Strong rationale for change

Staff in these schools clearly understood the reasons for changing curriculum and instruction practices. They examined their beliefs about teaching and learning, discussed what the curriculum should be, developed a strong rationale for changing business as usual, and decided upon implementation and assessment strategies. This important process provided the foundation for their actions. The "why" question had been addressed, answered, and thoroughly understood. We believe that failing to conduct a full examination of the issues stated above is to guarantee that no real and lasting change will occur. To propose solutions without creating a need is to continue the "fad myth" in schools as the only model of change.

In Solon, newly integrated curriculum arose out of concerns about the traditional curriculum which did not fully engage all students in high level learning, as well as serious professional study of the emerging integrated curriculum literature. In Ashland, questioning about curriculum was a logical outgrowth of teachers' study of adolescent development and resulting curricular implication; solid and honest relationships on teams further allowed teachers to ask probing questions about curriculum. At McKelvie Middle School, a twenty year history with interdisciplinary approaches led to the next logical step of more fully integrated units which rapidly became THE curriculum, not merely another add-on. In these and the other schools, the question of "what's next" was an essential question in moving to curriculum integration. Having solved issues related to organization and school climate, each of these schools realized that there was something more to do. And the answer to that something more was in the attack on the curriculum itself.

The rationale for improving curriculum serves as the visible symbol of understanding, beliefs, and commitment. It is the foundation upon which opportunities are built for students. It serves to institutionalize the change so that it becomes an integral part of the educational structure. It resoundingly, for all to hear, answers articulately and comprehensively the question *why.* It forces us to do what we know makes sense. Finally, it justifies what people who work with young adolescents know to be true about teaching and learning.

Building a rationale for change is the first step that must be taken to change and improve learning for young adolescents.

Building a rationale for change is the first step that must be taken to change and improve learning for young adolescents. If we are ever to develop curriculum that is meaningful and relevant, we must start with a careful consideration of the criteria by which curriculum is developed and delivered. All too often we have instituted change without such analysis and thus our innovations have been viewed solely through the rather muddied perspective of traditional curriculum. If we wish to make education truly responsive to the changing needs of society and its individuals we can do so by paying close attention to goals and criteria at the outset. When the rationale for changing the criteria for success are absent, it is all too easy to hang on to the traditional, which succeeds under the only remaining criteria—survival.

A major factor in defining a rationale for changing the curriculum in each of the schools was the unique context surrounding it. The type of community, parental expectations, and community history all played important roles in why these schools were changing from traditional curriculum to something else. While the context for each was very different, there was an underlying belief in each case that the traditional curriculum was not offering the greatest opportunity for young adolescents to develop fully.

Real learning

One of the major criticisms of any type of curricular change that moves us away from conventional curriculum is that because it looks different from that which is familiar, it must not involve serious and high-level learning. Could this criticism come from those with a very limited view of what constitutes learning? The traditional school model—separate subject classes, seven period days, teacher talk and student response, tests, and other school regularities—is recognized and regarded by nearly everyone as THE model by which all other models are judged, and newer models which require more student involvement, more hands-on learning, and more student responsibility are regarded with some suspicion.

Students in the seven situations described are involved in learning which looks very different from what passes as learning in many traditional schools. At Garland Street Middle School John Kraljic's students in Technology Education identify their own areas of study, work cooperatively on them and reflect on the entire process. Students at Timothy Edwards Middle School work on a month-long genealogy project which culminates in a Family History Celebration attended by 500 grandparents, parents, and children. Students at Brown Barge Middle School pursue "streams" or themes both in cooperative groups and in individual tasks. They are fully engaged using discovery learning as well as direct instruction.

These examples graphically illustrate learning in integrative settings that varies dramatically from the "show and tell" mentality of conventional schools. Integrative curriculum offers more rigorous opportunities for learning than the conventional school curriculum. Students who work in an integrative curriculum find challenging, intellectual learning, not "academic place-keeping."

Change—not feared

Not surprisingly, all of these schools involved in changing the conventional curriculum did so in different ways, at different points in their development as a middle level school, and, of course, for a variety of different reasons. They all began with a "do-able" task and realistic expectations of what they could do. Only one set out to totally "restructure," to totally overthrow what was currently being done and invent a new way of doing things. Largely, given the structures and parameters of their schools, each changed from within. This is an important lesson.

Individuals in these schools are risk-takers, particularly in one important area—they did not wait for all questions to be answered before they began their particular project. A critical point, which all discovered, is that, as the Nike slogan advocates, they just had to "do it."

Curriculum change is hard work and is not for everyone.

There is rarely a magical movement when the planets are aligned or where a higher being urges us on. When it comes down to it, we must begin change at some point, even when things may appear to be satisfactory with the present system. Change must be of the heads-up, straight-ahead type, where one realizes that risks must be taken. This point requires special emphasis: curriculum change is hard work and is not for everyone.

Teachers in the Blue Valley District in Kansas started with multidisciplinary units which led to more fully integrated offerings; John Kraljic at Garland Street Middle School just decided to try it to see if some degree of integration would work; teachers at Solon decided to "go for it" after doing their homework on what was appropriate for young adolescents.

So much of the literature on change strategies is contradictory. Some authorities recommend going as far as you can at the beginning, but going slow enough so that you don't alienate too many people or leave them behind. Other change agents recommend to "push the envelope" as far as you can initially, because large changes become increasingly more difficult with time. Still others suggest starting small, or involving everyone, or involving only those ready to change, and on and on. Although precise change prescriptions are unclear, what is clear is that doing must accompany thinking!

The most critical point for these schools is that they started. They did something and did not allow inertia, state or district standards, or parental concerns to hold them back.

Strong administrative support

Almost without exception, these schools had administrative leadership that was strong and supportive of teachers' efforts. Principals saw their roles as active participants, philosophically committed to integrated curriculum. Their assistance included encouraging exploration and risk-taking.

When you have a group of professionals who are willing to take a risk, support is needed. Including administra-

tors into the thought process for developing the rationale
behind moving to an integrated curriculum gets them in on
the ground floor which allows for support all along the way.
(Charlene Carper)

When roadblocks occurred, the administration would remove them or assist the staff in finding ways to go around them. They lessened the burdens of
organizational constraints. For example, they helped with scheduling by providing more flexibility in time for teams. They viewed the schedule as submissive
to the curriculum, not the other way around. They also provided time in addition
to regular team planning time. They recognized that curriculum change is hard
work, and as such they looked for ways to encourage, not discourage efforts.

With parents, principals were cheerleaders, leading the information campaign to keep them abreast of activities. They also encouraged parents to be
physically involved when possible as members of extended teams. They func-
tioned as front-line players, answering questions and verbally supporting efforts.

It's a continuing communication issue with parents.
It's a concept so foreign to parent's experience, yet they
hear from the media the need for students to make connections. We have to educate parents on a policy basis.
(Charlene Carper)

Principals provided staff development opportunities for their teachers. If
teachers needed more information or training, they found a way to provide it.

They also assisted in the identification of staff needs. In many instances
they helped problem-solve with the teachers. This proved to be a critical piece.
Not only were they viewed as the administrators, but were seen as
someone who had a stake in their success. Principals were seen as
valuable resources, allies not adversaries. They stayed involved throughout all phases—planning, implementation, and evaluation.

Principals were seen as valuable resources, allies not adversaries. They stayed involved throughout all phases.

Finally, and probably most important, they recognized the inherent personal dangers that teachers encounter when they take a risk.
Teachers place themselves in a fragile state, not only subjecting themselves to scrutiny from outside the system, but serious questions from colleagues
within. Any attempt to alter the curriculum, much less such a bold attempt as
this, surely makes all players in the school uneasy and cautious. There is even
the peril of other staff attempting to undermine their efforts as a defensive strategy, for if the innovators are successful, the ramifications for the rest of the
faculty are significant.

The day to day lives of these risk-takers can be very stressful. These principals, through their actions and comments, demonstrated an understanding of, and appreciation for, these efforts. That was probably their most significant contribution in supporting the changing curriculum.

Students learn content and more

Most are familiar with the work of Gordon Vars, long-time professor at Kent State University, who examined over 200 research studies (1992) comparing the results of integrated curriculum approaches with traditional separate-subject approaches. Vars found that schools using integrated approaches had similar or better achievement than did those schools with a traditional curriculum and instructional system. Reports from the schools included in this book are consistent with Vars' findings.

For example, Solon indicated that all but two percent of its students meet course objectives on a consistent basis. In Ashland, all teachers responding to the question about how much they thought students learned using an integrated approach as compared to the traditional programs, indicated students had learned as much, with 60% of them believing they had learned more. Timothy Edwards Middle School, using the Connecticut Mastery Tests in grade six and eight, has demonstrated an increase each year in students' scores and it has also seen a gradual increase in the number of students who get all A's and B's.

In addition to the achievement data, schools have been able to assess and demonstrate student growth in other areas. For example, some schools reported a decline in the number of discipline referrals and an increase in attendance when the students are involved with integrated units. Students report their enjoyment with real life learning and having an active part in the process. They indicate being able to see connections between subjects. Students, also, state that they like the opportunity to work with other students, often with groups they were not scheduled to be with in the past. Learning has become relevant, fun, and rewarding but also rigorous. This may prove to be the greatest attribute to continued success in school.

Whether by teacher-made exams, standardized tests, or authentic assessment strategies, these schools have been able to document learning. A key will be disseminating the results from new evaluation strategies to the community, thus reassuring them that their children are learning. This task is difficult, as adults, unfortunately, have come to measure learning by SAT scores, achievement tests, and report cards with letter grades.

It will be necessary to continue to give information on how students are achieving academically even as we are in the process of redefining what is academic. The task is monstrous and filled with peril. We must, as Laura Boutilier states, "balance our efforts on pure academics with what we know is right, always making sure to articulate to the public the degree to which outcomes are being met." Schools must document success if they are to get the support of a skeptical public to continue their important work.

Schools must document success if they are to get the support of a skeptical public to continue their important work.

Schools use a variety of assessment strategies and reporting systems

> Assignments which only ask students to memorize facts and formulae no longer prepare them for tasks that confront them as adults .
> (Teacher, Brown Barge Middle School)

New ways of organizing and delivering curriculum call for new ways of thinking about how we measure what students are learning. This initially may mean the use of a dual assessment system, one to monitor the old curriculum and teaching strategies and a new one that goes beyond paper and pencil learning. This need to develop different assessment methods creates a double pressure for staff. Not only are they working to create new learning opportunities but they often feel caught between reliance on traditional forms of assessment, which don't work but which the public assumes are accurate indicators of student performance, and searching for new strategies which are reliable, valid, possible to do in terms of time, and simple enough to be understood by the public and skeptical staff.

The dilemma is indeed complex, frustrating, and often filled with trial and error excursions. This is in stark contrast to the ease and stability of using publisher-developed or standardized test items which primarily assess knowledge recall and low level concepts, and are simple to administer and score.

What these schools shared in common was a willingness to explore new ways of defining and assessing student outcomes and of reporting that to parents. Although the schools used paper and pencil tests, they also used student performances, projects, portfolios, productions, journals, simulations, technology, experiential learning activities, parental input, student feedback, community service, and other alternative strategies.

Solon Elementary School from the beginning documented learning through district-wide standardized tests, state assessment tests, as well as analysis of individual student performance. At McKelvie Middle School, teachers developed new reporting systems such as the midterm progress report ,which provides information on specific activities of the unit under study, along with quiz and test scores, and affective elements of the unit.

The examples in the school stories chapters are benchmark activities. Although we can observe pieces of these authentic assessment techniques in other schools, what sets these schools apart is the fact that their assessment results are consciously related to a different curriculum approach. The rationale is clear. It is not just an attempt to evaluate the old curriculum in a trendy manner. Different assessment techniques applied to the old curriculum do not change the curriculum. What is recognized in these schools is that all change is systemic, that to change one piece of the school, the curriculum in this case, without changing the way it is assessed, does not make sense.

These schools also recognize the significance of collecting and analyzing data. Data are collected, compiled, and analyzed to assist in curriculum evaluation. It is in this later area that the most significant information may be gathered. Schools are not historically known as institutions where meaningful mechanisms are in place to provide formative and summative program evaluation information. Terry Despres, Ashland School, stressed the need for not only documenting success to respond to critics but supporting the continued development of new ideas by staff.

To change the curriculum without changing the way it is assessed does not make sense.

Seeing success gives the staff the inspiration and courage to continue. They know their efforts are paying off. For too long staff only knew intuitively or from an occasional comment if they were successful. For years we have shortchanged staff, students, and the community because of inadequate evaluation systems. These schools are showing us that to implement a new curriculum without providing ways to assess its effectiveness is not only foolhardy, it's professionally shortsighted and counterproductive.

High performing teams

Teams that go above and beyond are paramount. A lot of time is necessary for designing and continually refining every year. It's not like using a textbook. Teams must be able to work together on a continued basis not just on one product.

(Charlene Carper)

Although the teams in these schools were at various stages of development they all had one characteristic in common—they all worked hard at being a team. They had to learn to work together, make decisions collaboratively, and compromise. They struggled with the notion of functioning as a team while still maintaining individual member identities. At times, this caused conflict as roles were unclear. As teams became more unified, they began to use each member's talents, recognizing that all needed to have a stake in the team's success. Curriculum change is difficult as teachers often equate their identity and worth with what they teach. When subject lines become fuzzy, an individual's status within the school or team can be challenged.

Unless there are procedures in place for reaching consensus, promoting collaboration, and reducing conflict, curriculum issues will never be addressed seriously. These teams established operating norms which allowed them to work closely together, even (perhaps especially) when they disagreed. Also, successful team work was recognized by the principal as imperative to curriculum change, and attention in the form of staff training was provided to support this belief.

Unless there are procedures for reaching consensus and promoting collaboration, teams will never address curriculum issues seriously.

In all the schools, except Brown Barge, teams and students stay together for at least a year, and in some cases many years. At Brown Barge Middle School they change every trimester. Teams are reconfigured based on the streams developed, as well as faculty expertise. In essence, teams are ever-changing. This certainly creates unique and unusual problems in team development. As principal Barr notes, "teams have to learn how to compromise and reach consensus particularly when the teams are fluid." At Brown Barge, data indicate that students like changing teams because it gives them opportunities to meet and work with students they wouldn't come in contact with if they were on a fixed team.

High performing teams are essential if any kind of meaningful curriculum change is to be made. Effective teams require and nurture a tolerance for varying ideas. Just as we recognize student diversity in curriculum development, so should we honor and nurture it in adults. Adult teams must work cooperatively even though this concept of cooperation is foreign to most educators by their own preparation and experience. Camille Barr states it powerfully when she comments:

> Modeling cooperative group behavior for students is one of the single most important responsibilities we have as teaching professionals. How can we expect them to work successfully in groups if we can't.

Time for planning and coordination

Time is a critical factor, and each of these schools recognized the need to find time to study, plan, implement, and evaluate the changes they made. Quite

A major hinderance to change is the lack of time (perceived and real) to study, discuss, and make improvements.

possibly one of the largest hinderances to change is the lack of time (perceived and real) to study, to discuss, and to make improvements.

What often happens is that in the midst of some sort of change, teachers feel compelled to continue the old way of doing things as well as add on the newer changes. This rarely works because you can't have it both ways. You can't continue with the old curriculum while attempting to integrate it in a newer manner. This results in a great deal of frustration and usually ends with, "I knew this would never work, it takes too much time."

Planning time is crucial. Business and industry have long recognized how crucial research and development time is to their future success, Schools have rarely given much value to researching practices. These schools knew that to make the changes of the magnitude they imagined, they had to find planning time which would allow them to do this serious work. While before school, after school, and summer curriculum work are traditional answers to the time dilemma, these schools used in-house substitutes, release days, and other creative time-saving measures to literally "buy" the planning time they needed.

Students involved in planning

One of the major questions looming on the curriculum integration horizon is "What is the appropriate level of student involvement?"All of the curriculum projects presented in this book involve and engage students in their own learning to a much greater extent than traditional classrooms.

In several instances, students had choices of activities and topics for the first time but responded to the curriculum work done previously by their teachers. In other schools, students were intimately involved in the process of defining what their curriculum would be and in pursuing activities which allowed them to satisfy that curriculum. At McKelvie Middle School, while teachers had long recognized the engagement of students in interdisciplinary studies, it took several years before teachers realized that this type of enthusiasm would be more consistent with a totally integrated curriculum.

Meaningful student participation and involvement begets more involvement! Students at Garland Street Middle School readily admitted that they were unprepared for the responsibility which they were given, but they also acknowledged how important it was for them to have those responsibilities. As one student said, "the next time around I will take full advantage of those opportunities."

The real value of curriculum integration is in allowing students to become actively involved in setting their learning focus. The more authentic student involvement, and the more that involvement is valued, the more engagement in their own learning will occur.

Curriculum has a problem focus

Without exception, schools in this study either began with or are moving to a student-centered curriculum based on the problems and issues of young adolescents. As a point of contrast, note the schools which have started at one end of the continuum as they move from a traditional classroom toward the beginnings of multidisciplinary units. In these cases multidisciplinary units are usually topical—Sports, Holiday Celebrations Around the World, or Whales—rather than themes, such as environmental survival, transitions, or relationships which allow greater breadth and depth of study.

Themes with a problem focus are preferred because they allow a tremendous range of responses from a variety of students, all of whom may attack the problem from a different point of view tied to interest. Topics are somewhat limiting, even when they engage students more than is traditional. In fact, there may be a sort of Hawthorne Effect when moving from traditional to multidisciplinary units. And there is great concern that the themes, questions and overall study in such units will be unfocused, haphazard, and lacking in any kind of coherent plan.

The other problem with topics rather than themes, is that quite often topics are chosen from the textbook or curriculum guides without regard for their importance or usefulness in the larger curriculum. In other words, sometimes under the guise of interdisciplinary units, we perpetuate the traditional curriculum, albeit in a more palatable form.

Humans are a problem-solving species and there are certainly a large number of problems to be solved. When left to their own devices, young adolescents will choose problems which are relevant to them, both personally and in a larger world context. These schools took advantage of that interest and motivation to strengthen their curriculum. Virtually all of these schools are moving from teacher selected units to student selected units.

When left to their own devices, young adolescents will choose problems which are relevant to them, both personally and in a larger world context.

Parents and community involved

One of the largest issues schools face when integrating curriculum is explaining the process to parents who are more familiar with the conventional curriculum and its perceived benefits. It is critical, we think, that teachers and administrators NOT underestimate the importance of involving parents and community members in serious curriculum discussions, because we know that curriculum integration past the lowest levels will rarely occur without parental support. On the other hand, parental criticism of the curriculum can seriously wound change efforts.

Support in these schools for the curriculum changes they made was mixed. And judging from the reactions in other communities, it is safe to say that as schools move further along the curriculum continuum, away from the conventional, parent and community concern will escalate.

The experiences of the Cardigan Project at McKelvie Middle School show the benefits of long-term parent support generated from direct parent participation in all phases of the project. Most of these schools involved parents in culminating events from integrated units—the Family History Celebration at Timothy Edwards Middle School, various units at Solon Elementary School, and the Energy Fair at Ashland. While such events are important and provide a visible sign of the work being done, teachers must be careful to explain these types of projects as culminating events in a larger process of learning; we don't want parents to see these types of activities through the lens of "this is a nice science activity, now let's get back to the important book work!"

It is critical that a discussion of integrated curriculum begin with a larger discussion about what teachers, parents, and students value and expect from school. Talking about curriculum integration will convince few people about its efficacy, but demonstrating it to them will be much more effective.

It's hard work and not for everyone

Curriculum change is not for the timid. For many it is a whole new way of doing business. You have to be comfortable with the notion of not always getting it right and not always knowing exactly where you're going.

> This has been a leap of faith, but not a blind leap. We are convinced that it's the single most important contribution we can make to middle school reform in the country.
> (Camille Barr)

It takes time—more than is usually allocated. Some regular team planning time should be designated for curriculum work while extra time will also be needed.

Change evolves slowly. It calls for a change in beliefs about who can learn and what they should learn. It calls for changes in the roles of teachers and students in the curriculum process.

Although the premises and rationale of integrated curriculum are understandable, logical, and without much argument, they are still difficult to accept. Hence, some aren't ready to make the leap. Even though outside the school their personal lives are current, within the schoolhouse they are content with living in the past. What they would not tolerate in their personal lives, they are comfortable with at school. Such teachers and administrators live a dual standard and are not ready for curriculum change.

Those who develop and implement curriculum have to be risk-takers, not content with accepting the status quo. Rather they seek to redefine the status quo. They work beyond traditional expectations and are driven to make learning more meaningful and relevant for students. On occasion they are chastised by fellow teachers, small groups of parents, and administrators. However, they have the courage to continue because they believe strongly that what they are doing is right and is making a difference. →

REFERENCES

Achievement of U.S. students debated. (March, 1993). *Curriculum Update, 35*(3), 1, 4-5. Association for Supervision and Curriculum Development.

Aikin. W. (1942). *The story of the eight year study.* New York: Harper and Row.

Alexander, K., Cook, M., & McDill, E. (1978). Curriculum tracking and educational stratification: Some further evidence. *American Sociological Review, 43,* 47-66.

Alexander, W. (1962). What educational plan for the in-between-ager? *The NEA Journal 55* (March), 30-32.

Alexander, W., & George, P. (1981). *The exemplary middle school.* New York: Holt, Rinehart & Winston.

Alexander, W., Williams, E., Compton, M., Hines, V., & Prescott, D., (1986). *The emergent middle school.* New York: Holt, Reinhart & Winston.

Apple, M. (1968). *Teachers and texts.* New York: Routledge and Kegan Paul.

Arnold, J. (1980). Needed: A realistic perception of the early adolescent learner. *Clearinghouse 54* (Winter), 4.

Arnold, J. (1985). A responsive curriculum for emerging adolescents.*Middle School Journal, 16*(3). 14-18.

Arnold, J. (1990). *Visions of teaching and learning: 80 innovative middle level projects.* Columbus, OH: National Middle School Association.

Arnold, J. (1993). A curriculum to empower young adolescents, *Midpoints 4:1,* Columbus, OH: National Middle School Association.

Atwell, N. (1987). *In the middle: Writing, reading, and learning with adolescents.* Upper Montclair, NJ: Boynton/Cook Publishers, Inc.

Bailey, T. (1991). Jobs of the future and the education they will require: Evidence from occupational forecasts. *Educational Researcher, 20*(2), 11-20.

Barker, J. (1988). *Discovering the future.* (Videotape).

Beane, J. (1975). The case for core in the middle school. *Middle School Journal, 6* (Summer), 33-34.

Beane, J. (1976). Options for interdisciplinary teams. *Dissemination Services on the Middle Grades, 7,* 1-6.

Beane, J. (1987). Dance to the music of time: The future of middle level education. *Schools in the Middle,* 1-8.

Beane, J. (1990a). *A middle school curriculum: From rhetoric to reality.* Columbus, OH: National Middle School Association.

Beane, J. (1990b). Rethinking the middle school curriculum. *Middle School Journal, 21*(5), 1-5.

Beane, J. (1991). The middle school: The natural home of integrated curriculum. *Educational Leadership, 49*(2), 9-14.

Beane, J. (1992). Turning the floor over: Reflections on a middle school curriculum. *Middle School Journal 23,* 34-40.

Beane, J. (1993a). Problems and possibilities for an integrative curriculum.*Middle School Journal, 25*(1), 18-29.

Beane, J. (1993b). *The middle school curriculum: From rhetoric to reality* (2nd ed.), Columbus, OH: National Middle School Association.

Beane, J. & Lipka, R. (1986). *Self-concept, self-esteem, and the curriculum.* New York: Teachers College Press.

Beane, J., Toepfer, C., & Allesi, S. (1986). *Curriculum planning and development.* Boston: Allyn & Bacon.

Becker, H. (1990). Curriculum and instruction in middle grade schools. *Kappan 71* (February), 450-457.

Belasco, J. (1991). *Teaching the Elephant to Dance.* New York: Crown Publishers.

Bilodeau-Jones, M., & Bossie, J. (1993). Integrated studies in a multi-age classroom at the middle level: You can get there from here. *Journal of the New England League of Middle Schools, 6*(3), 8-11.

Block, S. (1985). *Belief systems and instructional improvements: A lesson in mastery learning.* Paper presented at the annual meeting of American Educational Research Association, Chicago, IL.

Braddock, J. (1990). Tracking the middle grades: National patterns of grouping for instruction. *Kappan, 71*, 445-449.

Brazee, E. (1987). Exploration in the "regular" curriculum. In E.N. Brazee (Ed.), *Exploratory curriculum for the middle level.* Rowley, MA: New England League of Middle Schools.

Brazee, E. (1989). The tip of the iceberg or the edge of the glacier. *Mainely Middle, 1* (Spring), 18-22.

Brazee, E., & Capelluti, J. (1992a). Integrating the curriculum: A look at two programs. *NELMS Journal, 5*(3), 20-23.

Brazee, E., & Capelluti, J. (1992b). Middle level curriculum: Making sense. *Middle School Journal, 23*(3), 41.45.

Brazee, E., & Capelluti, J. (1992c). Middle level curriculum: Just do it! NELMS Journal, 5(2), 26-28.

Brazee, E., & Capelluti, J. (1993a). Curriculum integration: Getting out of the blocks. *NELMS Journal, 6*(1), 25-29.

Brazee, E., & Capelluti, J. (1993b). Why an integrative curriculum for middle level: A recent rationale. *NELMS Journal, 6*(3), 21-27.

Brazee, E., & Capelluti, J. (1993c). Focus on middle level curriculum: Frequently asked questions about integrative curriculum. *NELMS Journal, 6*(2), 25-27.

Brazee, E., & Capelluti, J. (1994). The curriculum continuum: Getting where we need to be! *Journal of the New England League of Middle Schools, 7*(1), 1-6.

Brodhagen, B., Weilbacher, G., & Beane, J. (1991). Living in the future: An experiment with integrative curriculum. *Dissemination Services on the Middle Grades, 23, 1-7.*

Burke, W. (1982). *Organizational Development: Principles and Practices.* Boston: Little, Brown and Company.

California State Department of Education. (1987). *Caught in the middle.* Sacramento, CA: Author.

Caine, R. ,& Caine, J. (1991). *Making connections: Teaching and the human brain.* Association for Supervision and Curriculum Development.

Capelluti, J., & Eberson, J. (1988). What makes one Maine middle school successful? *Journal of Maine Education, 4*(1), 52-55.

Capelluti, J., & Eberson, J. (Eds.). (1990a). *Change in education: Strategies for improving middle level schools.* Rowley, MA: New England League of Middle Schools.

Capelluti, J., & Eberson, J. (1990b). Parent/student exchange day. *Middle School Journal, 21*(4), 8-9.

Capelluti, J. & Mundry, S. (1990). *Change in education: Strategies for improving middle level schools.* Rowley, MA: New England League of Middle Schools.

Capelluti, J., Eberson, J., & Mundry, S. (1991). A successful middle school: Can it be replicated? *NELMS Journal, 4*(2). 3-5.

Capelluti, J., & Stokes, D. (Eds.). (1991). *Middle level education: Programs, policies, & practices.* Reston, VA: National Association of Secondary School Principals.

Carnegie Council on Adolescent Development. (1989). *Turning points: Preparing American youth for the 21st century.* New York: Carnegie Corporation.

Commission on Standards for School Mathematics, (1989). *Curriculum and evaluation standards for school mathematics.* Reston, VA: National Council of Teachers of Mathematics.

Compton, M. (1984). Balance in the middle school curriculum. In J.H. Lounsbury (Ed.). *Perspectives: Middle school education, 1964-1984.* Columbus, OH: National Middle School Association.

Corbett, D., & Blum, R. (1993). Thinking backwards to move forward. *Kappan, 74*(9), 690-694.

Council on Middle Level Education. (1984). *An agenda for excellence at the middle level.* Reston, VA: National Association for Secondary School Principals.

Council on Middle Level Education. (1989). *Middle level education's responsibility for intellectual development.* Reston, VA: National Association for Secondary School Principals.

Dewey, J. (1956). *The child and the curriculum/The school and society.* Chicago, IL: University of Chicago Press. (Originally published in 1902 and 1900, respectively.)

Drahe, S. (1991). How our team dissolved the boundaries. *Educational Leadership, 49*(2), 20-24.

Eichhorn, D. (1966). *The middle school.* New York: The Center for Applied Research in Education.

Eichhorn, D. (1972). The emerging adolescent school of the future-now. In J.F. Saylor (Ed.). *The school of the future-now.* Alexandria, VA: Association for Supervision and Curriculum Development.

Eichhorn, D. (1992). *Why middle schools. Middle level education: programs, policies and practices.* Reston, VA: National Association of Secondary School Principals.

English, F., & Hill, J. (1990). Restructuring: *The principal and curriculum change.* Reston, VA: National Association of Secondary School Principals.

Epstein, J., & Mac Iver, D. (1990a) The middle grades: Is grade span the most important issue? *Educational Horizons, 68*, 88-94.

Epstein, J., & Mac Iver, D. (1990b). National practices and trends in the middle grades. *Middle School Journal, 22*(2), 36-40.

Erb, T., & Doda, N. (1989). *Team organization: Promise practices and possibilities.* Washington, DC: National Education Association.

Findley, W., & Bryan, M. (1975). *The pros and cons of ability grouping.* Bloomington, IN: Phi Delta Kappa.

Fogarty, R. (1991). Ten ways to integrate the curriculum. *Educational Leadership, 49*(2), 61-66.

Fullen, M., & Hargreaves, A. (1991). *What's worth fighting for in your school?* Toronto: Ontario Public School Teachers Federation.

Gamoran, A., & Berends, M. (1987). The effects of stratification in secondary schools: Syntheses of survey and ethnographic research. *Review of Educational Research, 57*, 415-435.

Gardner, H. (1983). *Frames of mind: The theory of multiple intelligences.* New York: Basic Books.

George, P. (1993). *Tracking and ability grouping: Ten tentative truths.* Unpublished manuscript.

George, P., & Oldaker, L. (1985). *Evidence for the middle school.* Columbus, OH: National Middle School Association.

George, P., Stevenson, C., Thomason, J., & Beane, J. (1992). *The middle school and beyond.* ASCD.

Goodlad, J. (1984). *A place called school.* New York: McGraw-Hill.

Guskey, T. (1981). Measurement of the responsibility teachers assume for academic successes and failures in the classroom. *Journal of Teacher Education, 32*, 44-51.

Hoffman, J. (1991). Speech at New England League of Middle Schools, Hyannis, MA.

Huelskamp, R. (1993, May). Perspectives on education in America. *Kappan 74* (9), 718-721.

Integrating the curriculum. (1991). (Theme issue). *Educational Leadership, 49*(2), 4-75.

Integrating the curriculum. (1989). (Theme issue). *Educational Horizons, 68*, 6-56.

Jacobs, H. (Ed.). (1989a). *Interdisciplinary curriculum: Design and implementation.* Alexandria, VA: Association for Supervision and Curriculum Development.

Jacobs, H. (Ed.). (1989b). Interdisciplinary curriculum options: A case for multiple configurations. *Educational Horizons, 68*, 25-27, 35.

Johnson, D., & Johnson, R. (1975). *Learning together and learning alone: Cooperation, competition and individualization.* Englewood Cliffs, NY: Prentice-Hall.

Johnson, M. (Ed.). (1980). *Toward adolescence: The middle school years.* 79th Yearbook of the National Society for the Study of Education. Part I. Chicago: University of Chicago Press.

Johnston, J.H. (1990). *The new American family and the school.* Columbus, OH: National Middle School Association.

Johnston, J., & Markle, G. (1986). *What research says to the middle level practitioner.* Columbus, OH: National Middle School Association.

Lake, S. (1988). *Equal access to education: Alternatives to tracking and ability grouping.* Practitioner's Monograph #2, Sacramento, CA: California League of Middle Schools.

Lipsitz, J. (1984). *Successful schools for young adolescents.* New Brunswick, NJ: Transaction.

Lounsbury, J. (1984a). *Middle school education: As I see it.* Columbus, OH: National Middle School Association.

Lounsbury, J. (Ed.). (1984b). *Perspectives: Middle school education. 1964-1984.* Columbus, OH: National Middle School Association.

Lounsbury, J., & Clark, D. (1990). *Inside grade eight: From apathy to excitement.* Reston, VA: National Association of Secondary School Principals.

Lounsbury, J., & Johnston, J.H. (1985). *How fares the ninth grade?* Reston, VA: National Association of Secondary School Principals.

Lounsbury, J., & Johnston, J.H. (1988). *Life in the three 6th grades.* Reston, VA: National Association of Secondary School Principals.

Lounsbury, J., Marani, J., & Compton, M. (1980). *The middle school in profile: A day in the seventh grade.* Columbus, OH: National Middle School Association.

Lounsbury, J. & Vars, G. (1978). *A curriculum for the middle school years.* New York: Harper & Row.

Maeroff, G. (1990). Getting to know a good middle school: Shoreham-Wading River, *Kappan, 71*, 504-511.

Marzano, R. (1988). *Dimensions of thinking: A framework for curriculum and instruction.* Alexandria, VA: Association for Supervision and Curriculum Development.

McDonough, L. (1991). Middle level curriculum: The search for self and social meaning. *Middle School Journal, 23*(2), 29-35.

Middle Level Curriculum Project. (1993). Middle level curriculum: In search of self and social meaning. In T. Dickinson (Ed.), *Readings in middle school curriculum. A continuing conversation.* Columbus, OH: National Middle School Association.

National Association for Core Curriculum. (1985). *Core today! Rationale and implications.* (3rd ed.). Kent, OH: Author.

National Middle School Association. (1992). *This we believe.* (rev.ed.) Columbus, OH: Author.

Noland, T. (1985). *The effects of ability grouping. A meta-analysis of research findings.* Unpublished doctoral dissertations, University of Colorado, Boulder.

Oakes, J. (1985). *Keeping track: How schools structure inequality.* New Haven: Yale University Press.

Pace, G., (Ed.). (1994). *Whole learning in the middle school: Evolution and transition.* Norwood, MA: Christopher-Gordon.

Pogrow, S. (1993). Where's the beef: Looking for exemplary materials. *Educational Leadership, 50*(8), 39-45.

Polite, M. (1992). *The story of Cross Keys middle school: Learning to ask the right questions.* Project Report: The National Center for School Leadership: University of Illinois at Urbana-Champaign, College of Education.

Romberg, T. (1993). NCTM's standards: A rallying flag for mathematics teachers. *Educational Leadership, 50* (5), 36-41

Rosenbaum, J. (1980). Social implications of educational grouping. *Review of Research in Education. 8*, 361-401.

Sarason, S., & Klaber, M. (1985). The school is a social situation. *Annual Review of Psychology, 36*, 115-140.

Sergiovanni, T. (1986). Understanding reflective practice. *Journal of Curriculum and Supervision, 1*, 353-359.

Sharpes, D. (1974). Unpublished curriculum guide. Reston, VA.

Siu-Runyan, Y.; and Faircloth, V. (Eds.) (in press). *Beyond separate subjects: Middle school curriculum for the 21st century.* Norwood, MA: Christopher-Gordon.

Silvernail, D. (1990). *A re-analysis of the construct validity of the responsibility for student achievement questionnaire.* Gorham, ME: University of Southern Maine, Center for Applied Research and Evaluation.

Silvernail, D., & Capelluti, J. (1991). An examination of the relationship between middle level school teachers' grouping preferences and their sense of responsibility for studes outcomes. *Research in Middle Level Education,* Columbus, OH: National Middle School Association, *15* (1), 21-29.

Slavin, R. (1987). Ability grouping and student achievement in elementary schools: A best evidence synthesis. *Review of Educational Research, 57*, 293-336.

Slavin, R. (1990). Achievement effects of ability grouping in secondary schools: A best-evidence systhesis. *Review of Educational Research, 60*, 471-500.

Slavin, R., Braddock, J., Hall, C., & Petza, R. (1989). *Alternatives to ability grouping.* Baltimore, MD: Johns Hopkins University, Center for Research on Effective Schooling for Disadvantaged Students.

Springer, M. (1994). *Watershed: A Successful Voyage Into Integrative Learning.* Columbus, OH: National Middle School Association.

Stevenson, C. (1986). *Teacher as inquirers: Strategies for learning with and about early adolescents.* Columbus, OH: National Middle School Association.

Stevenson, C. (1992). *Teaching ten to fourteen year olds.* White Plains, NY: Longman.

Stevenson, C., & Carr, J. (Eds.). (1993). *Integrated studies in the middle grades: Dancing through walls.* New York: Teachers College Press.

The Edison project. *Education Week.* (February 2, 1993).

Thomason, J., & Thompson, M. (1992). Even if it isn't broken: A proposal for wholesale change. *Middle School Journal, 23* (5), 10-14.

Valentine, J., Clark, D., Nickerson, N., & Keefe, J. (1981). *The middle level principalship.* Reston, VA: National Association of Secondary School Principals.

Van Hoose, J., & Strahan, D. (1988). *Young adolescent development and school practices: Promoting harmony.* Columbus, OH: National Middle School Association.

Van Til, W., Vars, G., & Lounsbury, J. (1967). *Modern education for the junior high school years.* Indianapolis, IN: Bobbs-Merrill.

Vars, G. (1992). *A bibliography of research on the effectiveness of block-time, core, and interdisciplinary team teaching programs.* Kent State University, Unpublished.

Vars, G. (1993). *Interdisciplinary teaching in the middle grades : Why and how?*(2nd ed.). Columbus, OH: National Middle School.

Wagner, T. (1993). Improving high schools: The case for new goals and strategies. *Kappan, 74(9),* 698-699.

Wang, M., Rubinsten, J., & Reynolds, M. (1985). Clearing the road to success for students with special needs. *Educational Leadership, 42,* 62-67.

Wigginton, E. (1985). *Sometimes a shining moment.* New York: Doubleday.

Wolf, D. (1987). *Portfolio.* The Arts Research Project.

Yager, R. (1987). Problem solving: The STS advantage. *Curriculum Review, 26*(3), 19-21.

Yager, R. (1988). A new focus for school science: S/T/S. *School Science and Mathematics, 88,* 181-190.

Yager, R. (1993). Science/technology/society—addressing the real problems in science education. *NASSP Curriculum Report, 22(3).*